Francesco Monicelli

Photography
Cesare Gerolimetto

Ville Venete

The Villa Civilization in the Mainland Dominion

arsenale editrice

Ville Venete
The Villa Civilization in the Mainland Dominion

Francesco Monicelli

Photography
Cesare Gerolimetto

Translation
Lemuel Caution

Graphic layout
Arsenale Editore

Editorial coordination
Silvia Scamperle

Printing
EBS Editoriale Bortolazzi Stei,
San Giovanni Lupatoto, Verona

First Edition
October 2012

Arsenale Editore Srl
Via Monte Comun, 40
37057 San Giovanni Lupatoto (Vr)
www.arsenale.it
redazione@arsenale.it

Arsenale Editrice © 2012

ISBN 978-88-7743-373-2

Contents

> *If Venice's arising from the sea might seem almost miraculous, by no means less extraordinary is the phenomenon of villas interspersed throughout the entire Veneto region, a singular phenomenon not only considering their numbers, but also their variety of aspect, the wealth and quality of the frescoes, stuccoes and statues with which they are decorated.*

Giuseppe Mazzotti
(introduction to the "Venice in the Countryside" exhibition, March 1978).

Bepi Mazzotti was one of those who, in the 1950s, brought the "civilisation of the villa" to world renown, investigating one of the fundamental aspects of Venetian history. This aspect was seriously running the risk of being obliterated thanks to the neglect and ignorance to which it had been condemned. The theme of the Veneto villas is a complex and fascinating one, and it unravels into the multiple facets of government during the Veneto Domination of the Mainland: the relationship between the process of human colonisation of the territory and its environmental characte-ristics, historical-artistic values, the micro-history of families and communities, social repercussions, the problematics linked to the conservation and restoration of an imposing heritage, despite the losses that have unfortunately occurred over the centuries. Attempting to understand the reasons behind the countless villas that connote towns and countryside in the Veneto region requires a cursory glance at the historical reasons that led Venice to *cultivate the land after having cultivated the sea.*

Opposite page: panoramic view of 16th-century Villa Piovene Porto Godi, Lonedo, by Lugo Vicentino.

Historical Premises

*Above: Renaissance three-light window,
La Colombina, Isola di Carturo.*

*Opposite pages: aerial of Castello Grimani
Marcello, now Sorlini, Montegalda.*

The Origins of Venice

March 25th, in 421, is the legendary date for
the founding of Venice, when Alaric's Goths
and Attila's Huns arrived in the north-
eastern provinces of Italy and swarmed into
the Po Valley, forcing the inhabitants of the
coastal towns of the then dissolved Western
Roman Empire to flee towards the labyrinth
of the lagoon in the upper Adriatic. But 421
is much more closely linked to myth than
reality. In fact, it is with the arrival of the
Longobards in the mid-6th century that
the Veneto islands are transformed from
temporary refuge to urban settlement. As a
peripheral *locus* within the Byzantine system
which had survived Barbarian invasions,
from the very outset Venice played the
dual role of mercantile centre with naval
interests stretching into the lagoon and
along the river into the Po Valley and as the
distribution point for goods from the East.
Venetian historiography has it that the first
Doge was elected in 697, thus marking
independence from Byzantium. But in fact
the collapse of the Ravenna exarchate in
741, under pressure from the Longobards,
speeded up the lagoon islands' emancipation
from Byzantine domination.
This heralds the beginning of Venice's
thousand-year history. Venice quickly
became a sort of city-state, governed by an
oligarchy that was proud of its mercantile
origins and that jealously guarded its
independence, free of the influence of royal
and papal influence. The Veneto patriarchate,
scornful of noble title and feudal rights,
proud of constituting its own *fons honorum*,
politically committed and responsible for
the governing of the Serenissima Republic,
formed the founding basis of the political
and economic power of Venice and its
colonial empire which, at its height,
included the conquest of Constantinople
in 1204, predominance in the East and
extended, in different historical periods,
along the eastern coast of the Adriatic and
included the Peloponnesus, or "Morea"
as it was known, and the islands of the
Aegean and Mediterranean, amongst which
Candia, or Crete, Negroponte, or Eubea,
and Cyprus. At the crossroads of the Eastern
and Western worlds, in the Middle Ages
Venice represented the greatest emporium
that Europe had ever seen. The profits and
interests of the Republic were gradually
identified with the economic profits and
interests of the families that owned ships
and staples; from the 13th century, for three
hundred years, in fact, Venice was to play

the role of hegemonic commercial centre for all European countries and for the entire Mediterranean basin, to all extents and purposes a monopolistic regime governing the Eastern market. The Gold Ducat or "Zecchino" was introduced in 1284 and constituted the highest economic authority in the Mediterranean area right up to the modern period, and remained stable for five centuries in terms of its gold content and weight. This is the Serenissima's period of greatest splendour: it was the terminal port for all international traffic of the period, and its commercial and financial undertakings were so sophisticated that the merchant-patrician developed and honed insurance and associative forms that were able to improve the way companies were run and limit the risks they ran. Like Venetian banking institutions, the city's shipyards were unrivalled. The imposing Arsenale complex, a state-run shipyard, was one of the greatest concentrations of specialised labour in the Middle Ages. Proof of its efficiency was to be seen in the Spring of 1570 when, in only two months, one hundred galleys were built for the fleet that, in 1571, would defeat the Turks at Lepanto. But Venice's economic predominance and the Republic's pre-eminent political position were undermined in the 16th century when trans-oceanic navigation burgeoned following the discovery of the Americas (Venice was too geographically decentred to take part), with the advance and consolidation of Ottoman power in the Middle Eastern region and the onslaught of an ever-present piracy.

The consequence of this situation, which certainly showed no signs of changing over the years, was the systematic transformation of capital originating in mercantile activities into investments in real estate. The situation was further favoured by the consolidation,

*La Cordellina, Montecchio
Maggiore, built 1735-1760 by the Venetian
Giorgio Massari.*

from the mid-14th century on, of the Veneto's domination of the mainland, when Venice began to gain power over the territories controlled by the *Signoria*.

The land state

On the mainland, the change from the communal to the seigneurial order in the main cities had already taken place following the consolidation of the power of large feudal families such as the Romanos, Caminos, Carraras, Camposanpieros, d'Estes and Sambonifacios, names deriving from the castles owned in the countryside. From a strong aristocratic tradition founded on military strength, which appeared able to impose order within and security on the outside, the representatives of the large families were sometimes elected to *podestà*

offices or as captains of the people, positions that became permanent and hereditary with the involution of the *comunale regime*. In short, this is how the foundations were laid for the new *signoria* order. Important families were the da Caminos, *signori* in Treviso from 1283 to 1312; the d'Estes, who, with the help of Venice (granted on the proviso that the family limit its area of economic influence), extended their control to Ferrara in 1240; the della Scalas, a small noble family who were subsumed to the pinnacle of a large clan and who established their control in Verona between 1260 and 1277, when the Ezzelini family lost its control. Cangrande II della Scala's attempt to gain control of the entire region led to the election in Padua in 1318 of Jacopo da Carrara to the office of Captain General, thus giving rise to the power of

the Carrara family. Then, with the death of Gian Galeazzo Visconti from the plague in 1402, Francesco Novello da Carrara began his hegemonic rise to power (Gian Galeazzo Visconti had ousted Antonio della Scala from Verona in 1387). Venetian reaction was almost immediate. Venice feared any attempt to unify the Veneto mainland, and was particularly worried by the commercial vocation of Padua and its proximity to the lagoon; Venice, after all, wanted strategic and fiscal control of all routes to and beyond the Alps.

In 1405 Francesco Novello was defeated, captured, imprisoned and then secretly strangled. *Omo morto non fa più guera* ("A dead man no longer wages war") said his executioners, who then went on to eliminate all male members of the family. And to ensure their domination over the Mainland. After centuries, the fractured nature of the Veneto area between the lagoon, that is the city-state of Venice, and the hinterland was unified, and the disconnectedness of political communities competing with each other came to an end. The Mainland's definitive dedication, or rather submission, to St Mark towards the mid-15th century gave rise to a period of relative prosperity, with economic and demographic growth such that during the following century the central provinces of the Dominion (i.e. the current Veneto area) had a population of 1.2 million inhabitants.

In 1560, Venice itself had a population of 160,000. Of the other Veneto cities, only Verona was to reach the high-water mark of 50,000 inhabitants in particularly

Villa Velluti, Sambruson di Dolo, on the Naviglio di Brenta.

Rare 18th-century brickwork statue, Villa Zanchetta, Baggi di Rosà.

Next page. 18th-century Villa Balladoro Malfatti, Nesente in Valpantena.

prosperous years. Padua was in decline, and its population oscillated between 40,000 and 30,000 inhabitants. Vicenza had little more than 20,000 inhabitants, while Treviso and Chioggia had almost 15,000 and other urban centres were small towns with 5-8,000 inhabitants. The Mainland Dominion, which was constituted by a territorial complex which was anything but homogeneous, was subdivided into four parts: Istria, Friuli and Marca Trevisana (with Treviso, Belluno, Feltre, Padua, Adria and Vicenza), and Lombardy (with Bergamo, Brescia, Crema and Verona). Venice held on to the more important and profitable manufacturing activities, while the Dominion cities developed less economically important sectors, specialising in market areas that were functional to the capital. The Dominant city imposed unity, law and order: in exchange, it demanded "dedication", and maintained political and military control. Power, in fact, was entirely in the hands of a restricted Venetian oligarchy who gave very little leeway to the old governing elite of the Mainland, who had been demoted to *nobiltà suddita* (i.e., "the subjected nobility"). The *Podestà* and captains, the so-called rectors, present in the main cities with the *Camerlenghi* or Chamberlains, that is officials responsible for collecting taxes, and other minor officials, as well as *Podestà* and lords who controlled the municipal councils in the smaller cities and the fortifications strewn throughout the territory, were culled exclusively from the patrician class. Even the most important ecclesiastical offices, such as the bishoprics, archbishoprics and abbacies, were the exclusive domain of Veneto patricians. Venice thus gained control of the civic as well as religious sentiment of both the clergy and general population, and a line of defence for Venetian policy within the Apostolic See. The cities' councils continued to administer the distribution of taxes and land valuations, thus allowing local families with representatives to look after their own interests; at the same time, central government had no desire to

limit the extension of feudal jurisdiction, which was at times granted to particularly deserving subjects. But state political control was firmly in the hands of the Venetian patricians who, albeit conceding a few offices to the *nobiltà suddita*, resolutely held on to the reins of powers. The process of political assimilation and co-governance which the former local aristocratic classes had fostered was thus rejected.

The subjected nobles were not allowed to go about armed unless they were granted specific permission; members of the patrician families and subjected nobility were able to marry only in the closing decades of the Serenissima, even though they were very rare indeed for many centuries. Landed property was subdivided into the categories of *fuochi veneti* ("Veneto *foci*"), that is those lands belonging to patricians or citizens resident in Venice, and *fuochi foresti* ("alien *foci*"), that is all other landed property, including property belonging to the subjected nobility. There were also immense cultural differences: the patricians were used to handling problems of international politics from the East by dealing with legations to kings, emperors and popes, and managing vast financial operations; the vast majority of subjected nobles had rarely even left the confines of their city walls or their feudal areas of responsibility.

The Patricians

Who were the patricians who belonged to the restricted Venetian aristocracy and who defined themselves as *Veneto nobility*, those who proudly bore the title of *Nobil Homo Veneto* ("Noble Veneto Sire") and *Nobile Dama Veneta* ("Noble Veneto Lady"), those who, in documents, were referred to with the abbreviations of N.H. and N.D. before their names?

The right to this privilege was founded on the individual's belonging to the Republic's Maggior Consiglio, the sovereign political assembly responsible for electing the

Doge's electors and members of the other magistratures. The 1297 reform, during the reign of Doge Pietro Gradenigo, with the so-called *Serrata del Maggior Consiglio* ("The Lock-Out of the Maggior Consiglio") admitted only those who were current members of the Consiglio and those who had been members in the preceding four years, subject to approval by the *Quarantia* or *Consiglio dei Quaranta* ("The Council of Forty"). New candidates had to be vetted in the same way. Membership of the Maggior Consiglio became permanent and hereditary in 1323. Families were divided up into two categories: the "old houses", that is those who existed before the 9th century and derived from the ancient tribunes of the first communities, four of whom were known as "Evangelists" as they had founded the convent of San Giorgio Maggiore, and twelve were known as "Apostolic" as they were thought to have participated in the election of the first Doge, Paoluccio Anafesto, in 697; the "new houses", that is those who emerged after the 11th century and up to the Serrata del Maggior Consiglio. In 1381, after the war with Chioggia in which Venice was counterposed to Genoa, a further thirty families were added. These were known as the "Nuovissime" ("The Very New"), and had distinguished themselves by donating funds for the defence of the state. After this, admission to the patrician class was ostensibly no longer possible.

Others were co-opted only for honorary purposes. This was reserved for members of princely families such as the Gonzagas, Estes, Sforzas, Medicis and Savoias, foreign princes such as Henri III of France who visited Venice in 1574, or for the nephews of popes so that they had the juridical appurtenances needed to obtain ecclesiastical benefits within the Veneto state. Some of the families of the subjected nobility were also co-opted in order to reinforce specific political bonds, as happened with the Savorgnan family, who in 1420 promoted the submission of Udine to Venice. These, however, were isolated cases, and granted only external prestige and in no way permitted the family to participate in the state's public life.

The Republic's choice was substantially to demarcate the limits between social classes and to adopt a marital and hereditary policy the aim of which was the conservation of wealth, property and power. From 1506 patricians were obliged to register the birth of their offspring at the registrar's office in the *Avogaria di Comun* (the Municipal Advocacy), the future *Libro d'oro* (Golden Book); for male children, this meant they could be admitted to the Maggior Consiglio on their 25th birthday. This right was granted all male children (barring those embarking on an ecclesiastical career). They also inherited in equal part any wealth or property, which was often bonded in testamentary trusts. Unlike the rest of Europe, in fact, "Germanic law" with its primogeniture rights had not been adopted in Venice. Female offspring were only given dowries, which were inherited by male offspring; if there were no children, the dowry returned to the woman's original family.

In 1526, registration was made compulsory for marriages as well, thus reinforcing the endogamous nature of patrician society. In fact, any male child born of a woman from servile or plebeian classes was excluded from the Maggior Consiglio, and therefore from any political role. The consequences for any society based on endogamous principles, that is where marriages can take place only within the same social class or family group, are that the birth-rate inevitably drops.

If in 1570 there were about 2,500 25-year-old males registered in the *Avogaria di Comun*, in 1631, after the plague, there were only about 1,600. This patrician demographic crisis was accompanied by a state political crisis brought about by a lengthy conflict with the Sublime Porta in 1645, which would force the Serenissima into three expensive wars to maintain its domination over Candia, the Peloponnesus and the Ionian islands.

The costs of war could not even be covered

Detail of façade with faux-architecture decorations, Villa Giauna, Altivole.

Opposite page. View of eastern façade, Villa Ottolini, now Pignatti Morano di Custoza, Custoza.

by the selling off of municipal lands and ecclesiastical goods. At this time, amidst great debate, bickering and opposition, the Maggior Consiglio pushed through legislation that "opened up" the *Libro d'oro* and therefore the co-opting of new families – and no longer according to social class, but to economic wealth. Families able to contribute to the Republic's coffers were signed up, provided they donated the hefty sum of 100,000 ducats, the amount required to arm and pay 1,000 mercenaries for one year. There would be 128 new patricians aggregated between 1647 and 1718, of whom one fifth defined as *original citizens*, that is Venetian residents already in the *Libro d'argento* (Silver Book) from which the Republic's civil servants were culled and whose women were allowed to marry patricians, one fifth subjected nobles,

Pages 18-19: detail of the part of the building added in the year 1740 by Andrea Tirali to the body of Villa Duodo in Monselice designed by Vincenzo Scamozzi in 1589.

Opposite page: Villa Polverini, now Canossa, Casale sul Sile.

and three fifths plebeians, that is merchants and entrepreneurs with no traditional lineage whatsoever. This, however, proved to be a purely temporary solution, even though power remained firmly in the hands of the forty "great" families who still managed to command votes in the Venetian assembly. Despite the fact that, during the 18th century, the differences deriving from the different cultural backgrounds between the older and newer houses tended to diminish, traditional distinctions between the different patrician classes (senatorial, judiciary, Barnabite) did persist.

At the end of the 18th century, the number of patricians on the Maggior Consiglio had fallen to less than 1,000, so few that an attempt was made to co-opt new families in 1775 – and this time not according to wealth but rather as a sign of official gratitude. This was official recognition, forty years after the request was made, of the *Consiglio Politico presentato al governo veneto* (Political Suggestion Made to the Veneto Government) put forward by the Veronese Scipione Maffei, in which he asked for the ranks of the capital's patrician assembly to be extended to representatives from the mainland Consigli. The reasoning was that this would grant equal dignity to all the nobles of the Dominion and their services to the state. A new decree in 1775, therefore, gave forty families from the subjected nobility the chance to accede to the patrician class, provided they could prove that their family's nobility went back at least four generations and that they had a high enough annual income to maintain a *status* that was in keeping with the *more nobilium*. This was a last-ditch attempt to integrate patricians and subjected nobility – but it came too late. Only ten families applied for the *supplica* procedure. The Republic, its propulsive force enfeebled and its main concern that of proposing the empty rites of its own mythology, had come to its end: in 1797, Napoleon only had to add his name to an historical period that had already run its full course.

The villa settlements

Four centuries had passed since the Serenissima had conquered the Mainland, and during these 400 years the *pax veneta* had been interrupted only by the crisis brought about by the Cambrai war that began in 1509 when Agnadello was defeated and came to a close with the Conference of Bologna in 1529. In this period, Venice had bestowed resources and investments on the hinterland, creating appropriate arms of the magistrature, such as the *Provveditori sopra i beni inculti* (Superintendents for Uncultivated Lands) in 1556 and the *Provveditori sopra i beni comunali* (Superintendents for Municipal Goods) in 1574, setting up enormous projects for land drainage, so as to defend the lagoon from being land-filled, recuperating water-logged terrains for agricultural purposes, making as many river routes navigable as possible, with the voluntary or involuntary help of proprietors, and exporting culture, fashion and life-style. During these four centuries, the patricians' landed possessions covered enormous swathes of the territory that could be easily reached from Venice through a complex hydrographical network put together by the Venetian state. For example, in the Polesine district, which had become part of the Republic in 1482-1484, 95% of the land belonged to the Venetian patricians. There was also a very high percentage of land owned by the Venetian nobility in the Dogado district, the area from Grado to Cavarzere that represented the limits of the ancient Byzantine province, as well as in the Treviso and Padua areas; the percentage was lower, yet still rather high, in the Friuli district, which officially came under Venetian influence in 1445. Large tracts of land were also owned by Venetian patricians in the Vicenza valley area, in the Cologno district and in the southern Verona district. The percentage was much lower in the Belluno area, mainly because it was considered barely important in economic terms; the same was true for the provinces of

Brescia and Bergamo, which were difficult to reach via river, and were considered to be too distant. Here the local nobility played a major role in the countryside, and they were supported by local statutes that prohibited the selling of land to non-locals. There was also a high percentage of land owned by municipalities and institutions such as hospitals, schools, churches and convents. A very low percentage was owned by the subjected nobility who owned only 18% of the large landed possessions as opposed to the 32% owned by patricians. The lands themselves came from royal landed possessions which had, *ipso jure*, passed to the state, as well as from possessions confiscated from the old *signorie* families such as the Scaligeris and Carraresis, to which must be added those of the partisan families such as the Viscontis, or those who sided with the Empire during the Cambrai wars. Over time, the market was further added to by municipal lands as well as assets from religious congregations, whose hereditary rights the Serenissima had

radically curtailed. There were also repeated secularisation decrees for abbeys and convents. The government offices handling the state's demesne were the *Camere Fiscali* (Fiscal Courts), which were to be found in all cities, and whose job was to sell off land to the highest bidder. Venetians and subjects obviously did not have the same purchasing power, with the former decidedly richer, even though the patrician class also included *houses with nothing to their name*, the so-called *bernaboti*, thus called because they were given their houses free of charge by the Signoria in Contrada San Barnaba. Some families, such as the Contarinis from San Trovaso and the Pisanis from Santo Stefano, eventually owned vast swathes of landed property, including mills, taverns and shops the rural classes depended on, and owed the "Singori" tithes and emphyteusis rights. After all, the imperative to concentrate all economic and political resources within the state's maritime power changed abruptly, with enormous consequences for the Venetian economy

and its customs. *Nobilomeni* and enriched merchants felt that investing in agricultural land offered economic security, and thus noble subjects and the new bourgeoisie acted accordingly.

The subsequent need for field-cultivation structures went hand in hand with the need to actually represent this new-found social prestige – the country residence therefore became one of the most accomplished manifestations of this *more nobilium*. The duty to supervise the running of the enterprise and control the influx and size of the yield thus gave sense to the fashion and rite of vacationing in the countryside, the periods for which coincided with harvest time. These "Signori", in fact, were present in the countryside from June 12th, the eve of the feast day of St Anthony or the beginning of the harvest, to the end of August, and from the feast day of St Francis on October 4th, to about November 10th, the end of the grape harvest. The Venetian carnival began after this date, and there were very few indeed who willingly stayed away.

The architecture

*Detail of 15th-century portico,
San Vito di Altivole.*

The first villas

What are the villas like, how did they come about, and how have these buildings, which constitute the most significant element within the new territorial structure of the Land State, been modified? We must bear in mind that from the 15th century the villa, as a country dwelling, became an Italy-wide architectural phenomenon, and eloquently expressed a change in attitude regarding the relationship between the city and the country.

During the first decade or so of the *villa civilisation*, already-existing buildings were most probably used. Thus castles and towers which had lost their original function were restructured. Throughout the 15th century, the towers, tower-dwellings and small forts dotting the countryside became the privileged sites for the first villa settlements. The lower floors of towers were adapted to dwellings, while the upper storeys were used to rear doves; the annexed buildings, originally used to house soldiers, were converted into shelters for animals, tool sheds and warehouses for foodstuffs.

There are other factors which we must also bear in mind. The farms of the period were composite, multifunctional units, self-sufficient microcosms; throughout the

centuries the functional sectors of the farm were much more radically altered than the residential sectors, whose basic typology was already set as early as the 15th century. Not to mention the towers which were adapted for civil use and those that Mazzotti called "villa-castles", that is castles which had been transformed into dwellings, such as the Montegalda, Monselice and Zevio castles.

The earliest 15th-century villa nucleus has been located in the smallish and compact constructions, with two-tiered roofing, with characteristic porticoed façades on the ground floor with corresponding single-lancet or multi-lancet windows on the upper storey. This typology is respected by Ca' Montagna in San Zeno di Montagna, Verona, with its front section punctuated by three porticoed arches on the ground floor and three gothic-styled single-lancet windows on the upper floor; Villa Capra Filippi in Carrè, Vicenza, with a five-span ogival portico; Casa Quaglia in Paese, Treviso, whose recent restoration has brought to light the porticoed ground-floor structure, a central three-lancet window and two lateral two-lancet windows on the upper floor, as well as the façade's decorations, a motif characterising the main hall in Ca' Montagna. Palazzo Contarini in Arquà Petrarca is another example with the same typology, as well as Villa Dal Verme in Finale di Agugliaro. In this case the influence of Venice, and its *fondaco* houses, is obvious in the proportions of the building and the sophistication of the decorations.

Other Gothic villas gradually assumed a markedly urban character in terms of the refined nature of the stonework and the proportions which were closely styled on the city *palazzo*. A very good example is Villa Portico Colleoni, in Thiene. The large five-lancet window in the centre of the façade on the *piano nobile*, the five-span portico on the ground floor and the Ghibelline crenellation crowning the building contribute to making this home one of the most prestigious in the entire region.

Another example of this typology is the so-called Palazzo dei Merli (literally "House of the Blackbirds") in Gazzo Veronese, completed by 1490 for Zan Andrea Montanari. Even here the Ghibelline crenellation along the eaves seem to symbolise the feudal-cavalier origins of the family, as it does in Pressana, in the slightly later villa of the noble Querini family, princes of the Island of Stampali in the Dodecannesus.

Flamboyant Gothic characteristics, typical of the capital's culture, are also present in Villa Mocenigo, Mirano; these same characteristics can be seen in the canonical houses in Casalserugo and Vigonza, as well as in many other buildings throughout the countryside.

The most prestigious example, however, is Villa Spessa in Carmignano sul Brenta, which was built in about 1480 on the site of a medieval castle by the Vicentine entrepreneur Giovanni da Quinto.

The change in taste from the Gothic to the Renaissance can be seen in Villa Buri di San Pietro in Cariano and in Villa Angaran dalle Stelle in Mason Vicentino, as well as in the more magniloquent examples of Ca' Impenta, just outside the eastern gates of Vicenza, and Villa già Buri in Isola Rizza in the southern Verona district.

One of the most well-conserved buildings is Villa Corner Dall'Aglio in Lughignano sul Sile, built about 1490, with its façade facing onto the river and characterised by a grounded five-span portico and an elegant four-lancet window on the *piano nobile*. This same scheme can be seen in the slightly later Villa Trissino in Cornedo Vicentino.

Another typology for the 15th-century Veneto villa is based on an archetype of a villa

La Ca' Dotta, Sarcedo

Villa Mercante Labia, Cologna Veneta.

Villa Soranzo, Fiesso d'Artico on naviglio Brenta.

with portico and loggia, often accompanied by an earlier full-bodied dove-tower. This typology is well-defined in the piedmont area from the Verona right up to the Belluno districts. In the earliest examples the internal planimetry is articulated according to a sequence of rooms running parallel to the distributive axis formed by the portico and loggia, where the stairway linking the two floors is external and flanking the two floors. There are many such examples: in the Verona district there are Villa Quintarelli in Torbe, Casa Serego Alighieri in Gargagnago, Villa Fasanara di Valgatara, Villa Del Bene in Volargne di Dolcè, Villa Sparavieri in Settimo di Pescantina, Villa Verità in Arbizzano, Villa Bertoldi in Negrar, Villa Selle in Fumane, Villa Ridolfi Cossali in Cavalcaselle, Villa Catterinetti Franco in Cologne, Villa Pavarana in Azzago, Villa Berretta in Mizzole, Villa Pavesi in Poiano and Villa Cartolari in Avesa.

The important examples in the Vicenza district are Ca' Brusà in Lovolo, Villa Piovene in Brendola, Villa Valmarana in Creazzo, Villa "Porto Usei" in Zugliano, Villa delle Cattane in Vicenza (which has unfortunately been modified), Loggia Valmarana in Valmarana and Villa Povegliani Dal Zotto in Longara di Vicenza.

In the Treviso area there are Villa Dal Zotto in Venegazzù, which is one of the earliest, Casa Callegari in Farra di Soligo; in the Belluno district there are the Castello dei Lusa in Lusa, the smallish Villa Villalta in Cart and the later Villa Tonello di Artén.

In truth, the villa with portico and loggia was to provide other noteworthy examples into the very late 16th century, and even into the 17th. The source for this typology can be found in convent architecture, even though in all honesty illustrious precedents can be found in the Venetian fondaco houses originating in Byzantine models. The examples in Venice are the Fondaco de' Turchi on the Grand Canal, which was once home to the Este and then the Pesaro families, and the equally interesting palazzi Da Mosto, Dandolo Farsetti and Corner Loredan.

Sixteenth-century renewal

With the defeat of Agnadello in 1509, which sanctioned the beginnings of the Cambrai crisis, Venice felt the need to re-found its state organisation by augmenting the state's presence on the mainland. It was only in 1516 that Maximilian I freed occupied territories from Imperial domination. The liberation was sanctioned by the Brussels Treaty of 1517, and later confirmed by the ensuing Peace of Bologna in 1529. The Republic was thus able to definitively control the mainland nobility and began to dismantle rebel strongholds. Direct control of agricultural land by the patrician class was then encouraged via a network of villa settlements, which progressively transformed the continental order and were a direct response to stimuli of an economic order as well as the need for direct political control.

Hence the *pax veneta* which followed the Cambrai conflict and the heretofore unimaginable sense of security within the Veneto state favoured the formation of large tracts of agricultural property. When corn and rice were introduced and cultivated on a large scale (in collaboration with the Botanical Gardens of Padua), the patrician class was so enthralled that from the mid-16th century the main investments undertaken by the large families concentrated on villas and what they represented in the economy of the period. Other contributing factors were the unfavourable commercial conditions determined by the Turkish conquest in the East and the fact that the main international trade routes had moved to the Atlantic and the North Sea.

All of this was accompanied by an extraordinary profusion of economic and agricultural treatises, in part based on Latin *"de re rustica"* authors, which ideologically re-evaluated villa life, as propounded by the humanist entrepreneur Alvise Cornaro in his writings. The villa was therefore also seen as a place of culture which took up the Roman's *otium*; after all, Classical culture inspired almost all of the most important pictorial cycles in the villas, and even the statues and ornaments for the buildings and gardens themselves.

With the 16th century, therefore, the Veneto villa underwent a substantial change in terms of its compositional language and

Above: Villa Marogna,
Nogara, obviously indebted to Giulio Romano
from nearby Mantua.

Below: Villa Piovene Porto Godi, Sarmego,
attributed to Vincenzo Scamozzi

building canons, which were mindful of the Renaissance conception that privileged symmetry and golden proportion, not to mention great attention to decorative apparatuses.

Actually, at the same time as Andrea Palladio introduced his "villa-as-temple" revolution in the mid-16th century, there was a consolidation of the Venetian typology of the fondaco house, with its tripartite floor plan and longitudinal central hall with smaller lateral rooms, from which the body of the staircase was made to derive. The almost cubical volume of the building is covered by a four-tiered roof. The *piano nobile*, with this same plan, is on the ground floor, and the second floor is reserved for purely domestic purposes, and was usually used to store grain. The layout of the openings on the façade marks out the tripartite structure of the internal plan, with the central room on the piano nobile taking its light from a Serliana or a three-lancet window, with balcony, which constitute the focal point of the façade itself.

There are many such examples: Villa Loredan in Sant'Urbano d'Este, Villa Wiel in Negrisia di Piave, Villa Raspi in Chirignago, Ca' Cornera in Paolino di Fratta, Villa Vitali and Villa Soranzo in Fiesso d'Artico, Ca' Moro and Villa Gradenigo in Oriago, Villa Grimani Morosini in Martellago, Villa Querini Stampalia in Mira Porte, Villa Venier Velluti in Sambruson di Dolo, Villa Labia in Cologna Veneta, Villa Mocenigo in Canda, Ca' Dolfin in Lendinara, Villa Priuli in Piove di Sacco and Villa Renier Cavalli in Pontecasale.

The idea is therefore established of a city house transferred to the mainland: *palazzi* facing onto the Grand Canal are paralleled by villas on the Brenta waterway, or the Sile or the Canalbianco. The intermodality between waterways and land routes is the functional characteristic that links city and country dwellings.

The increase in Venetian presence on the mainland obviously heralded the exporting of the capital's tastes and models.

At the same time, this typology is flanked by another, according to which the villa is a cubic structure with a four-tiered roof and the traditionally Venetian tripartite floor plan. To this is added a ground or

Villa Tonello, Artèn.

basement floor for domestic and storage purposes, a single upper floor used for dwelling, which is reached via an external staircase, and a further upper floor used for storing grain. Palazzo delle Trombe, as Villa Saraceno in Finale di Augugliaro is also known, is emblematic of this archetype. This archetype was to set the trend for the entire century, and is substantially to be found in most of Andrea Palladio's villas.

There are noteworthy examples in the Verona district, including Villa Cipolla d'Arco Sagramoso al Corno, near Bussolengo, Villa Fiocco in Sommacampagna, Villa Ricci Manni in Settimo di Pescantina, Villa Fenilon in Santa Lucia near Verona and Villa Fittanza (owned by the patrician Garzoni family) in Boschi Sant'Anna.

In the Vicenza area, besides Palazzo delle Trombe, we have Villa Piovene Porto Godi in Grumolo delle Abbadesse, which has been dated to the late 16th century and attributed to Vincenzo Scamozzi.

Another important example is the nucleus of Treviso villas of the same type, such as Villa Barbarigo e Calvi in Biancade, Villa Carrer in Candolè, and Villa Bressanin Vazzoler in San Pelaio. There are also many example in the Padua area, such as Villa Corner Miari in Urbana, Villa Mussato in Megliadino San Vitale, Villa Colpi in Altichiero, villa Leoni in Piove di Sacco, Villa Foretti in Saccolungo, and Villa Valentinelli in Villa Estense. The Polesine district houses Villa Salvioni in Pontecchio Polesine and Villa le Guarine in San Bellino di Rovigo. The same archetype has been deployed for Villa Pasqualini Canato in Arquà Polesine, which, however, is closer to Ferrara models than Venetian models in terms of its stylistic references. Villa Loredan in Campolungo Maggiore and Villa Viterbi in Mellaredo are the more important examples in the Dogado area.

These villas, where the façade openings are normally symmetrically organised, sometimes have a loggia instead of a three-lancet window, represented by the entrance doorway and the two lateral windows.

Examples of this format are Villa Giusti in Vendri, Villa Agostini in Cusignana di Giavera del Montello, Villa Corner Chiminelli in Castelfranco Veneto, Villa Roberti in Brugine and Villa Colonda Marchesini in Campagna Lupia.

Villa Querini Stampalia, Pressana.

With the consolidation of large agrarian funds owned by Venetians, the richest and most pre-eminent patricians felt the need to build dwellings that were reference points not economically, but also culturally and geographically.

Villa Badoer Giustinian in Roncade is a paradigmatic example of this ideology; the residence of the Barbarigo family in Noventa Vicentina is a later example.

Andrea Palladio

Villa architecture was renewed towards the mid-16th century thanks to the genius of Andrea di Pietro della Gondola, renamed by Gian Giorgio Trissino as "the Palladio", an allusion to the goddess Pallas Athene, protector of the arts.

Rather famous architects such as Giovanni Maria Falconetto, author of the summer residence of the Bishops in Luvigliano, Padua (finished by 1538), and Jacopo Sansovino, who supervised the building of Villa Pontecasale for the Garzoni family in 1540, were not able to impose their villa model, inspired by the homes of the "Ancients" and linked to the "modern"

language of the most renovated Roman architecture. The same was true for the Verona architect Michele Sanmicheli, whose villas have never been identified with certainty but who is remembered for his Scomparsa Soranza in Treville.

Andrea Palladio, of humble Paduan origins and Vicentine by adoption, was "discovered" by the humanist Gian Giorgio Trissino, who initiated him to Classcial architecture and introduced him to Vicentine and Venetian aristocratic circles. Palladio's projects, no small part of which were realised, brought about an unprecedented renewal that was to hold sway until the fall of the Republic. He maintained the traditional tripartite structure of the Venetian façade and floor plan, with variations on the theme in the central, longitudinal room, sometimes replaced by a room with a Latin or Greek cross floor plan. But it was his introduction of Classical models, with columns and pilasters, tympana and statues, reserved for the dwellings of land owners, which constituted the "sacred" novelty that was destined to satisfy the requests of the dominant classes, within the complex articulations of the society of the time.

Villa Saraceno, Finale di Agugliaro.

Villa Foscari, known as La Malcontenta, Mira

Villa Zeno, Donegal di Cessalto.

Villa Cornaro, Piombino Dese.

Apart from his Classical echoes, however, the novelty introduced by Palladio, which also included the economic valence of the villa settlement, was his accomplished and rational organisation of the lateral rural buildings, thought of as a completion and crowning, if not the premise itself, of the lordly dwelling.

His Venetian commissioners were Pisani, Emo, Badoer, Foscari, Cornaro, Barbaro and Zeno; subjected nobles Godi, Caldogno, Saraceno, Poiana, Trissino, Thiene, Almerico and Serego were, however, able to compete only theoretically with the powerful rich patricians in commissioning Palladio for villas.

Palladio understandably left an enormous number of works.

There were many who followed in Palladio's footsteps: the Vicentine Vincenzo Scamozzi, whose Rocca Pisana and Villa Molin alla Mandriola reproposed Palladio's villa-temple with a central floor plan, albeit in completely personal terms; Francesco Zamberlan who is thought responsible for Villa Morosini in Cartigliano; many nameless designers such as those responsible for Villa Chiericati in Grumolo delle Abbadesse, Villa Molin in Fratta Polesine, Villa Maldura in Rivella di Monselice and Villa Acquistapace in San Pietro in Cariano. But there were also others who refused to accept the dictates of Palladian Classicism and opted for the Mannerism of Giulio Romano such as Dario Varotari, who designed Villa Emo in Montecchia di Selvazzano, and the designers of Villa della Torre in Fumana and Villa Marogna in Nogara, where the large entrance doorways to the courtyard definitely pay homage to Romano's work. There is also the Catajo complex in Battaglia Terme, which was built in about 1570

Villa Pàsole Berton, Pedavena.

Page 32-33: view of unfinished peristyle, Villa Serego, Santa Sofia di Pedemonte, the most "Roman" of Palladio's villas.

by Pio Enea degli Obizzi and Andrea da Valle in imitation of a castle complex and interpreted according to the poetics of the period.

It must also be pointed out that this abundance of villa architecture was also accompanied, in the 16th century, by a renaissance in the other arts. Perhaps the most productive areas were painting, with authors of the calibre of Paolo Veronese and the no less important Zelotti, Fasolo, Battista del Moro, Bernardino India and many others, and sculpture, where Alessandro Vittoria was one of the most important artists.

The later centuries

By the early 17th century, Palladian renewal had lost its force and turned into the cold, decorous Academicism of the later Scamozzi. Villa Sandi in Crocetta del Montello (1622), designed by Andrea Pagnossin, one of the last of the Palladian successors, seems to put an end to the Palladian school. The new Baroque fashion, which arrived from Rome with its panoply of imagination, passion for

decorative detail and celebratory intentions, found followers in Venice of the calibre of Baldassare Longhena, one of the movement's foremost interpreters. It nonetheless took a long time for the new forms to be received in other cities of the Veneto Dominion. Longhena himself used more moderation when designing country residences and linked them to the environmental values of the landscape in order to satisfy his wealthy commissioners' need for holidaying and official hosting, exclusively for patrician families such as the Lippomanos, Pesaros, da Lezzes, Contarinis and Widmans. The lexis of Baroque expression privileged curved and interrupted lines, which Longhena adopted for a series of buildings characterised by elaborate frontons, such as Villa Pigafetta in Montruglio di Mossano, Villa Gradenigo Bianchi-Michiel in Bassano del Grappa, Villa Tiepolo Passi in Vascon di Carbonera, Villa Troyer in Fregona, Villa Mafei in Valeggio sul Mincio and Villa Recanati-Zucconi in Fiesso d'Artico.

The 1630 plague, however, put a temporary stop to production. Nevertheless, in the mid-17th century, despite the political crisis

and economic hardship brought about by the Porta conflict, there was a marked upswing, and new villas were built and restoration work and extensions to already existing buildings undertaken. We should not forget that the 128 means-tested families co-opted to the patrician class were eager to demonstrate their new-found *status*.

The more decentred areas of the Veneto, such as the Verona, Belluno and Polesine districts, continued with a different type of villa production which, albeit appreciable in quality, is scarcely important in stylistic terms. The same can be said for the Friuli area, where the rejection of more lavish forms lends greater severity to the buildings. In fact, the greatest homage to the Baroque on the mainland is the renovation and extension of the ostentatious complex in Piazzola sul Brenta, undertaken for the Contarini family.

On July 21 1718, Venice signed the close of the third depleting war against the Ottomans, and, even though Morea was lost, this signalled the end of the vast expense of the war.

During the 18th century, Venice experienced a progressive political and economic crisis with an enormous budget deficit. The mainland, on the other hand, was faring well.

The countryside benefited from the agricultural experiments promoted by rural academies, while the piedmont area was experiencing great entrepreneurial activity in the fields of paper and cloth manufacturing, textile and ceramic production.

The new economic vigour of the Land State throughout the 18th century could be felt in the competition between patricians and subjected nobles to build and restore a great number of villas, with results that were a lot more prolific than the preceding century and comparable to the 16th-century golden age.

However, it was now official entertainment spaces as opposed to purely domestic ones that were being privileged, with a genteel main building preceded by gardens laid out according to strictly-defined axes, framed by guest houses and livery stables – that is, the villas were now being decked out with all the accoutrements needed for genteel holidaymaking. Animal shelters and barnyards were no longer the villa's

Villa Lampertico, known as La Deliziosa, Montegaldella.

characterising elements: the annexed buildings connected with agricultural activity were hidden away, and preferably at quite a distance, from the residential complex.

Those demanding villas developed ever more refined and fashionable tastes, consequently leading to the emergence of architects able to satisfy these desires, which were often in keeping with Palladian tradition.

Incomparable architects therefore came to the fore: Francesco Muttoni, Ottone Calderari and Ottavio Bertotti Scamozzi, who worked mainly in the Vicenza district; Giorgio Massari, who was responsible for the Cordellina in Montecchio Maggiore and Villa Tamagnino Lattes in Istrana; the Veronese Alessandro Pompei, Ignazio Pellegrini and Adriano Cristofoli; the Venetians Andrea Tirali and Antonio Gaspari; the Paduan Girolamo Frigimelica; Francesco Maria Preti from Treviso; and Giovanni Miazzi from Bassano.

The 18th century may well have been a period of stagnation in terms of Venetian politics and prestige, but it nonetheless also provided some of the most grandiose examples of villas built for obviously wealthy patrician families.

The national villa in Stra, where Frigimelica and Preti worked on the reconstruction and extension of an older building, was seen as an apotheosis of one of the "grand families", the Pisanis, sublimated by Tiepolo's allegorical fresco on the ceiling of the main hall. The building is a veritable royal palace, and no longer simply a "villa" in the Veneto tradition. In the same way, the Marini family, who were co-opted into the patrician class on the basis of their wealth in 1651, renovated and completed their sumptuous dwelling on the 6,000-acre parkland in Passariano, Friuli.

The difference between the economic needs of an agricultural concern on the one hand and celebratory intent on the other became ever more marked. Construction above all followed the dictates imposed by the desire to create villas that were symbols of a family's social destiny, according to a conception

Above left: villa Viaro Giustinian, Vanzo di San Pietro Viminario.
Above right: villa Pellegrini alla Pellegrina di Isola della Scala.
Below left: villa Nani Mocenigo a Canda.
Below right: villa Lippomano, Monticella di San Vendemiano, attributed
to Baldassare Longhena.

Left: villa Pellegrini, by Ignazio Pellegrini, Castion;
right: villa Giovannelli a Noventa Padovana.

Villa Toderini, Codognè.

Villa Widman Borletti, Bagnoli di Sopra.

Above: villa Tiepolo Passi, Vascon di Carbonera.
Center: villa Mosconi Bertani, Nóvare, by Adriano Cristofali.
Below: unfinished Villa Grimani, Pontepossero, designed by Antonio Gaspari.

that, over the centuries, left behind the primitive politics of Venetians taking over the mainland and began to follow models that were closer to the lifestyle of aristocrats from the large European courts.

Epilogue

The fall of the Republic of St Mark in 1797 brought about changes that profoundly influenced the equilibrium between Veneto states, first and foremost the environmental equilibrium of the lagoon itself, which had previously been protected by the severest of Serenissima laws. The brief period of French domination, which was followed by the much longer Lombardy-Veneto Reign under the Austrian flag, led, amongst other things, to the affirmation of a ruling elite that was closely tied to the cultural values of a post-Revolutionary bourgeoisie and to a loss of Venice's economic and political pre-eminence in favour of other cities. This in its turn led to an ever more dramatic "patrician crisis". At the end of the 18th century, a good 90 families originally included in the Libro d'oro had died out; a further 50 were to disappear in the first half of the 19th century. Disappearing families, inability to react and oppressive taxation imposed first by the French then by the Austrian government put paid to large landed properties and

led to the economic prevalence of new entrepreneurs, or to representatives of the old ruling classes who were able to change with the times. The 19th century was a period in which many of the dwellings, some of which of fundamental importance such as the already-cited Villa Soranza in Treville (project by Sanmicheli; frescoes by Paolo Veronese), were demolished. On the other hand, others were restored, some were newly built and many of the formal gardens were turned into landscaped parks according to the newly-imported English fashion.

Giuseppe Jappelli, Giannantonio Selva, Giovan Battista Meduna, Giuseppe Segusini, Antonio Caregaro Negrin and Giacomo Franco are some of the more important architects who left their trace in the Neo-Classical and Eclectical styles of the new era. Tastes that go from the Neo-Classical rigour of Villa Cittadella Vigodarzere in Saonara and Villa Gera in Conegliano, to the Gothic touches of Villa Bonìn-Longàre in Montecchio Precalcino, the Renaissance tones of Villa Revedin-Bolasco in Castelfranco Veneto, the Moorish shades of Villa Musella in San Martino Buon Albergo, the "style compositions" of Villa Drigo in Mussolante and the "modernity" of Villa Giovannelli in Lonigo.

Above: composite façade, Villa Cittadella Vigodarzere, Saonara, designed by Giuseppe Jappelli, circa 1816.

Center: villa Franceschini, Arcugnana, built 1770 by Ottavio Bertotti Scamozzi, restored second half of 19th-century by Antonio Caregaro Negrin

Below: 16th-century Villa Calza, known as La Serenella, Montemerlo. Neogothic restoration undertaken post-1860 by Giuseppe Cecchini Pacchierotti (below right).

18th-century Villa Gritti, Fossolovara di Strà,
restored by Moschini family in the 19th century

16th-century Villa Sale di San Damiano Curti,
Sovizzo, with 1892 faux-architecture decorations

18th-century Villa Da Lisca, Busòlo di Vago di
Lavagno, with pronaos and wings added 1920s by
Guglielmo Guglielmini.

Page 42-43: view of Villa Negri,
now Piovene Porto Godi, Mussolente.

Ca' Marcello

Monselice

Above: articulated series of bodies forming oldest nucleus of Castello di Monselice.

Opposite page: Ezzelino tower seen from large courtyard.

The Romans developed the ancient *Mons Silicis*, a prehistoric, palaeo-Veneto settlement, along the slopes of Monte Ricco, as a *castrum* along the Consular route inaugurated by Lepidus in 173 BCE. During the Lombardy domination Monselice became an important political-administrative centre that extended to the outskirts of the city of Padua, to whom it later fell. It was then that the city walls, castle and public *palazzo* was built and the city was subdivided into four districts. In 1239, Ezzelino III from Romano, Imperial representative for Frederick II, reinforced the fortifications along the hill, known as the Rock, and the city walls, extended in the following century, during the territorial skirmishes between Verona and Padua, to include five orders of wall. It was thanks to the da Carrara family, who had risen to the top ranks of the Paduan signory, that many important additions were made and embellishments added to the castle. The castle is now a sort of compendium of different series of buildings that stretch from the late medieval period to the 16th century. When Francesco Novello da Carrara fell in 1405, Monselice came under the

Opposite page: detail of Venetian-Gothic three-light window in middle body built by Marcello family.

Below: façade of 18th-century seigneurial Santa Lucia chapel attributed to Andrea Tirali.
Below-right: articulated sequence of staircases along garden terraces, Ca' Marcello, restored 1930s.

dominion of the Serenissima, and the Rocca was divided into three lots and given to the three patrician families – the Marcellos, Malipieros and dei Duodos. It was the Marcello family who gained possession of the ancient Carrara castle, which they renamed Ca' Marcello, and were responsible for the upkeep of the area. The Marcellos were therefore responsible for the middle Venetian Gothic body of the building, with three-lancet window and Ghibelline crenellation bringing

together the so-called *castelletto* and the Romanesque house dating back to the 11th century, and the large trachyte block built by Ezzelino da Romano between 1249 and 1256. A portico was opened up on the front of the Carrara residence looking onto the courtyard. Then the entire area was fitted out with staircases linking the terraces and the parts of the house used

Opposite page: the Hall with old fireplace,
with monumental 14th-century fluted fireplace
had built by Francesco the Elder from Carrara.

Below: castle armoury, ground floor,
Palazzo Ezzelino.

by the guards on patrol. During the 17th century, in the further reaches of the garden, the Marcellos built a small *palazzo* to house their library (it would later house Vittorio Cini's), and where the *Antiquarium* is currently held with Longobard tombs found during recent excavations. Then, in the early part of the 18th century, the Marcellos brought the complex to a close when they built the noble chapel dedicated to St Lucy, and attributed

from his maternal grandmother and completely restored between 1935 and 1939. His consultant was Nino Brabantini, director of Venice's Civici Musei. Count Cini from Ferrara, one of the richest industrialists of the period and great collector and patron of the arts, wanted Ca' Marcello to be transformed into a residence *cum* museum dedicated to the golden age of the Serenissima. This is why the Monselice castle, bought by the

to the Venetian Andrea Tirali. The Marcello family owned the castle until 1835, after which it was bought by various families who gradually expropriated it of its contents and left it in a state of abandon during World War I. Ca' Marcello was then requisitioned and turned into an army barracks. Count Vittorio Cini must be given credit for rescuing the entire complex, which he inherited

Veneto Regional government in 1981, has one of Italy's best collections of decorative arts, including furniture, fabrics, tapestries, sculptures, paintings, weaponry and furnishings. Cini's restoration brought unity to the complex while respecting the different construction periods. A number of ornaments were added, such as the red Verona marble column-bearing lion and the large coat of arms on the

façade of Palazzo Ezzelino, which was originally over one of the Monselice city gates pulled down in the 19th century.

You can walk through the courtyard to the armoury, where the walls are covered in red and white checks, the colours of Carrara. Here you will find a collection of 15th- and 16th-century weaponry. The second floor houses the 16th-century apartment, whose six rooms were originally part of the Ezzelini home and filled with Renaissance furniture, paintings and fittings from various places. The third floor, which can be reached via a covered staircase, contains the large greeting hall with four Flemish tapestries by Cornelius Mattens. The most important room, however, is the so-called *Room of the Old Fireplace*, decorated with painted red and white checks and dominated by a monumental fireplace in the shape of a multi-tiered tower with little, multi-lobed arches over small majolica columns, probably commissioned around the mid-14th century by Francesco the Elder from Carrara. From the *Castelletto*, which faces onto the "Venetian" courtyard with its Gothic well-head and two sarcophagi from the Vittorio Cini collection, you can walk through to the Romanesque house, with its kitchens and Council Room. The Cini-Brabantini collaboration is obvious here as well. They are responsible for the atmosphere, mediated by the historicising interpretation of the era, the medieval fortress which the Venetians transformed into a Renaissance residence when they arrived. Well worth the visit are the external areas as well, with their secret gardens and belvedere terraces on different levels, and linked by staircases and passages.

Above: grand Hall, white-and-red chequered Carrara wall decorations.

Opposite page: detail of so-called Sala della Bifora, with priceless Flemish arras on wall.

Castello di Lusa

Lusa

Above: tower at Lusa in lush greenery of Feltre mountains.

Opposite page: western front of imposing Castello di Lusa, with evident 16th-century addition.

One of the east European invading forces that followed each other from the fall of the Western Roman Empire was that of the Longobards, who occupied the Feltre region between the mid-6th and late-8th centuries.

With the sack of Feltre, the leading families abandoned the city and sought refuge in their feudal country residences. One of these families was the Lusa family, whose name derived from the name of the castle in Cesio, built on a raised stretch of land between the Stièn and Caorme rivers and dominating the valley below along with two other castles belonging to the same family (Arsòn and Pullìr).

Two important Lusa nobles were Gorgia, an ally of the Verona Scaligeri family and nominated Bishop of Feltre and Belluno in 1327, and Girolamo, who in 1509 sided with the Venetians against the emperor Maximilian. Despite the fact that the advent of the Dominante (circa 1420) led to the dismantling of castles belonging to the local families, including the Lusas. Thus began a series of attempts to transform the castle into a residential villa, where, after the restoration and excavations demanded by the current owners, the different phases of construction undertaken in almost every single century were highlighted. It was thus discovered that the buttress between Stièn and Caorame was inhabited in the very remote past, as demonstrated by the protohistoric discoveries on the site.

The remains of very thick enclosing walls to the south, along with a moat and drawbridge, indicate a much larger fortified area than the one covered by current extant structures. Destruction caused by war or natural forces such as the earthquakes of 1117 and 1348 were always followed by restorations which eventually led to the current complex, which is formed by two counterposed blocks facing onto a courtyard enclosed within crenellated walls.

In the early 15th century, what was probably originally the keep and the adjoining building were transformed into a belfry, the defensive intent of which can be gleaned from the almost 1.5-metre thick walls. This was flanked by a three-arched loggia opening up onto the internal courtyard. Then, most probably after the Cambrai crisis, the villa was given its current form with portico and scalloped seven-

light loggia on squared stone pilasters, which, unlike other buildings, was covered in plaster.

This is also when the elegant single-light arches in the massive body of the tower were opened. Even the smaller building in front of the main building has interesting elements, such as the two-light arch in front which looks out over the sheer cliff, and the remains of internal frescoes, which have been dated to the first half of the 16th century. The circular rampart at the foot of the tower is from the following century, however, and testifies to the defensive role Lusa continued to play over the centuries. The old chapel was found along the slope down valley, situated outside the current courtyard but in the oldest fortified perimeter, of which there are now mere traces.

The interior of the villa was restored to its original function, which had been compromised by preceding restoration work – original elements were found and reintroduced, the rooms were reorganised so they led into one another, and were re-distributed along the axis formed by the portico and the loggia.

The early 16th-century completion of the portico and loggia structure was not undertaken by the Lusa family, but by the new owner, Donato Villalta, a famous physician who would give rise to the Bovio Villalta branch of the family. One of the members of this

family was Caterina, who in the mid-18th century married Paolo Zambaldi, a recently ennobled jurist. She and her husband made a series of changes to the villa, including opening up the two balconies in the loggia parapet, which had been eliminated in the preceding restoration.

The current owners' imposing restoration work has not only underlined the different constructive phases of the complex, but has also highlighted its Renaissance character and saved it from certain ruin (it had become a country hayloft).

Villa Porto Colleoni

Thiene

Opposite page: detail of Gothic entrance gate, Castello Porto Colleoni, with view of cupola, Thiene duomo.

Aerial view of Thiene Castle, with complex of service buildings. To the right, seigneurial chapel; to the left, large duomo with tower designed by Sebastiano Serlio.

You will have to use all your powers of imagination to envisage the monumental impact Villa Porto Colleoni must have had on Thiene and its surrounding fields. The central structure of the building, the crenellated coping and the high enclosing walls which led to its being called *The Castle* or *The Palazzo* must originally have defined the urban landscape of Thiene in a way that is no longer conceivable.

The ancient Porto family from Vicenza, whose noble privileges were conceded as early as 1082 by the emperor Henry IV, seems to have been installed in the city (as it was defined in 1492) of Thiene from the mid-14th century. Their landed property increased considerably over the following century. Then a rather large dwelling must have been built as early as the 14th century, perhaps on the site of the old Santa Maria castle, which harked back to the Ezzelini era. The current building was begun by Francesco di Bartolomeo Porto in the 1440s; it was then passed on to his son Giovanni, and was eventually handed down to Giovanni's nephew Francesco in 1507, a man of arms who was nominated Collateral General of

*Previous page: the severe façade facing
onto the river.*

*Opposite page: detail of the villa's main façade,
with elegant florid Gothic five-light window.*

Below: garden, the gallery.

the Republic by Doge Andrea Gritti in 1532. It was Francesco who undertook the most imposing of enlargement and embellishing work on the villa. According to recent studies, this work was completed around 1525 after the devastation of the Cambrai war.

In 1541, Francesco Porto put a constraining order on the property which, in the absence of direct heirs, went to his nephew Giovanni, who then called on Zelotti and Fasolo to undertake frescoes on the interior walls of the villa.

His son Giovanni Battista then had a fishing pond put in, as well as a citrus garden and a grotto designed by Cristoforo Sorte, one of Andrea Palladio's collaborators from Verona.

In 1816, on the death of Giovanni Battista Orazion, the last of the Porto di Thiene family members, the property and family name were inherited by Orazio Guardino Colleoni.

The villa was abandoned for thirty years, and it was only in about 1850 that a series of works on the building were begun. This is when embellishments such as the towers' salient crenellations and the garden were undertaken.

When Guardino Porto-Colleoni died in 1918 without any direct heirs, the villa was inherited by his cousin Antonio di Thiene; hence the castle became part of this family's patrimony, where it has remained since.

The building is predominantly late-Gothic harking back to 15th-century Venetian architectural models. This is most obvious in the main façade, which is opened up on the ground floor by a five-light portico with lancet arches on rectangular pilasters and an elegant five-light window on the *piano nobile*, flanked by two crenellated bodies with high, trumpet-shaped chimneys.

*Opposite page. 18th-century stable,
attributed to Francesco Muttoni.*

*Detail of entrance hall, with Neo-mediaeval
decorations undertaken during 19th-century
restoration.*

Walled swallow-tailed merlons also hedge in the middle section of the building, which was originally decorated externally with faux-tapestry patterns which can now barely be seen; the eastern section contained large warrior figures which have since disappeared. The back façade is similar to the main one as far as the lateral bodies are concerned, while the middle section, which contains no portico or loggia, regularly follows the layout set by the openings. All these elements make Villa Portico-Colleoni the most conspicuous of residential Gothic buildings on the mainland whose form and embellishments were derived directly from contemporary Venetian examples.

The ground-floor cruciform atrium and the room immediately above it have maintained their original size. The second room once contained a cycle of frescoes depicting worldly scenes, painted by Giovan Battista Zelotti towards the mid-16th century. In the same period, Zelotti and Giovanni Antonio Fasolo frescoed the *Camerone*, or large hall, on the ground floor, which still now contains a refined Lombardesque fireplace with poly-lobed hood, with a score of architectural elements including four scenes taken from the history of Rome. The implied theme is that of the opposition between faith and loyalty, as exemplified by Scevolus and Scipio, and betrayal, as exemplified by Antony and Cleopatra and the meeting between Massinissa and Sophonisba.

This was probably an allusion to the behaviour of the Porto family, who remained loyal to St Mark during the years of the Habsburg occupation of the Veneto.

Next to the side entrance to the villa, the Romantic garden contains a well-head, dated 1559 and attributed to Andrea Palladio; behind the building there is a grotto designed by Cristoforo Sorte in about 1579.

Above: view of large cruciform hall on the piano nobile, with paintings.

Below: detail of Lombardesque fireplace with poly-lobate hood in the so-called Camerone room.

Opposite page: detail of fresco in eastern portion of the Camerone, by Giovan Battista Zelotti and Giovan Antonio Fasolo.

Unfortunately, the fish pond and its statues of Diana and other deities are no longer extant. Among the surrounding buildings, the most interesting is the stable, probably built by the architect Francesco Muttoni in the first half of the 18th century. The stable building, with a wooden beam ceiling, is subdivided into smaller rooms for horses by long lines of red Verona marble columns topped by soft-stone statues of putti. The white and red marble floor and the original fodder-troughs are equally noteworthy.

Just in front of the main entrance, in the piazza, is a noble Gothic chapel dedicated to the Virgin Mary. The chapel, which was also used for public services, was built in the second half of the 15th century, and has two single-light arches flanking the portal. Next to this there is the old parsonage, with its Renaissance elements. This building is also known as "the little red house" because of the colour of the plaster.

Villa Giustinian
Ciani Bassetti

Roncade

Above: garden statues.

Opposite page: entrance bridge,
Castello di Roncade.

The Badoer family, one of the oldest in Venice and part of the twelve "apostolic" families who had elected the first doge in 697, boasted direct descent from Agnello Partecipazio, the doge elected after the Frankish invasion when the capital of the lagoon population had been established on the islands that now constitute modern Venice.

After the death of her first husband, Agnesina Badoer married the General Procurator Girolamo Giustinian. She inherited the lands her forebears had bought in Roncade, between the Piave and Treviso, and between 1511 and 1522 she decided to abandon the old lordly home, which is still in the town's main square, and move to a new home.

These were the years of the Cambrai war, which was certainly present in everybody's mind during the building of the new home. The main building was contained within a rectangular crenellated enclosure, in its turn surrounded by a large moat taking its water from the Musestre, an affluent of the Sile, with four enormous square towers at the four corners of the building, to which were added

two circular towers alongside the main entrance. The aim was obviously to highlight the strongly symbolic themes of feudal iconography, while at the same time respecting the real needs of defence from mercenaries and bandits, as can be evinced from the various trapdoors in the towers and the defensive *portello* on the Musestre at the strategic crossroads for Treviso, the area beyond the Piave and the riverside road for Altino.

The villa, on the other hand, is quite different. It is a prototype of architectural themes that would later

Left: the main façade of the villa with large fireplaces in tower.

Above: detail of gardens, with view of one of the two angular towers along battlement walls.

be taken up by Palladio, including the portico with overhanging loggia and the concluding triangular fronton. The building has a rather heavy parallelepiped shape which has been lightened by the addition of a jutting loggia with three superimposed arches, preceded by a small staircase and crowned with a fronton. The façade still contains the remains of a frescoed architectural motif which covered the compact volume from the house to the loggia. The villa was further embellished with the addition of two enormous chimneys in the

shape of towers, which were placed at the intersection of the folds of the roof. The classical forms of the building and numerous decorative elements, such as the arched windows encased within architraved frames, the string-courses and the elegant double-amphorae balusters along the loggia parapet, all indicate the anonymous architect's indebtedness to the Venetians Tullio Lombardo and Mauro Codussi. They also reflected the desires of culturally aware commissioners who were interested in keeping abreast with what was happening in the capital. The rear façade is less rigorously embellished than the main façade, and is mainly simplified because of its lack of string-courses, architraves above the window arches and the jutting loggia, which has been replaced with a large staircase and by a no-longer-extant arched pronaos held aloft by columns. The rustic components of the Roncade villa are adequately and rationally extended to the arched *barchesse* which are developed along the large entrance courtyard, which is divided by two low walls aligned with the façade and two large secret gardens to the sides and behind the villa. A portal, whose axis is aligned with the main building, can be found in the rear enclosing wall and gives onto the *brolo piccolo* (or small garden), a common element in 15th- and 16th-century villas and farmhouses, used mainly as a fruit orchard and for recreation.

The large courtyard in front of the house (originally used as a farmyard) was ennobled throughout the 18th century. Its original perspectival structure was punctuated by spires and stone spheres and statues of *ultramarine infantrymen or slaves* sculpted out of Istrian stone and attributed the Bonazzas' Paduan workshop. The cedars of Lebanon and large flowering magnolias, however, were planted in the 19th century, and were part of a general garden restructuring project that respected contemporary landscape tastes. There is also a noble chapel dedicated to St Anne, built between 1542 and 1543, to the left of the villa and attributed to Santo Lombardo, Tullio Lombardo's son. Here there are terracotta busts of the building's commissioners (Agnesina Badoer and Girolamo Giustinian), which their son Marcantonio had commissioned. They have been attributed to Jacopo Sansovino.

The villa itself still contains the original ceilings, Sansovino-like painted beams and frescoed friezes, as well as neo-Classical-style stuccoed decorations.

The Roncade villa remained the property of the Giustinian family until the death of Maria, the last of the family's descendents, in 1915. After her death, the villa was sold to the barons Ciani Bassetti who were responsible for restoring the villa after the damages it suffered in World War II.

Rich sculptural décor in front of the villa, with glimpse of the chapel façade.

Above: one of the ground-floor living rooms, with late-18th century stuccoes.

Ground-floor entrance, with bust of Doge Marcantonio Giustinian.

Villa dei Vescovi
Luvigliano

*Opposite page: detail of entrance gates,
with view of Villa dei Vescovi.*

*Above: the cubic mass of Villa dei Vescovi,
surrounded by the Colli Euganei.*

On a wonderful site in the heart of the Colli Euganei, where there was once a castle belonging to the powerful feudal Transalgardi family (destroyed by Ezzelino da Romano), there is now a historical summer residence built for Paduan bishops. As early as 1474 Bartolomeo Bon from Venice had accepted Bishop Jacopo Zeno's request and set about planning the villa, which, however, was soon interrupted. Building began again in the early 1530s, when the diocese was run by Cardinal Francesco Pisani, who had nominated *curial governor*, that is administrator of the bishopric, a certain Alvise Cornaro, who was to become one of the main figures in the villa's history and an emblematic player in the contemporary cultural field.

Cornaro (1475-1566), a non-noble Venetian and a patron of the arts and supporter of Ruzzante and Falconetto, was passionately devoted to the theatre, studied hydraulics and agriculture and had written a treatise on architecture, *Discorsi sulla vita sobria* (1558), where he exalted "holy agriculture" and provided a series of

practical suggestions for a healthy life-style which derived from the serenity of country life. Cornaro was therefore the main artificer behind the Luvigliano villa. He called Giovanni Maria Falconetto, one of the most renowned architects of the period. Falconetti (b. Verona, 1468) had begun his career as painter and antique dealer. Having sided with the forces of the Empire during the Cambrai wars, he moved to Rome when the Venetians regained power and studied architecture. Once he had been officially pardoned by the Veneto government he moved home once more, and was accepted by Alvise Cornaro. In 1524 he built a loggia for Cornaro in the courtyard of the Paduan home he had inherited from his uncle Alvise Anglieri, and in 1534 he was responsible for the so-called Odeo. Both these are reminiscent of the works of Bramante, Raffaello and Baldassare Peruzzi.

In 1540, on Falconetto's death, the Luvigliano villa was all but completed. Falconetto and Cornaro had planned to construct the villa on a showy quadrangular podium of about 45 metres per side. The villa was given a square floor plan of 38 metres per side, so as to leave room for large terraces around the building. The link between the *piano nobile* and the terracing was provided by two double staircases on the front and back of the building; the link between the podium and the *piano di campagna* was provided by spectacular multi-flighted staircases interrupted by jutting terraces. The floor with the living quarters had deep seven-arch loggias along the two façades. These loggias are punctuated by Doric pilasters which prop up the high trabeation, which is decorated with a frieze with stone triglyphs and rounded metopes. The arched plan is repeated, albeit with "blind" arches, along the sides of the front of the building. The lower floor, which provided the servants' living quarters, is covered with a delicately rusticated plaster. The noble floor was originally structured around a peristyle (harking back to Classical tradition); this was transformed into a walk-through hall in the early 18th century by the bishop Nicolantonio Giustiniani.

The living quarters are divided into two

Previous page: villa seen from the secret garden, with portico added by Andrea da Valle.

Opposite page. Southern portico with **trompe-l'oeil** *frescoes echoing surrounding landscape.*

Below: detail of villa arches.

Below-right: detail of entrance gate from southern loggia.

symmetrical apartments, in keeping with the traditional distinction between summer and winter apartments. These, however, were in all likelihood reserved for the bishop on the one hand, and guests on the other.

When the complex was completed in 1542, the frescoes were added along with stuccoes along the *piano nobile*, where, amongst the faux architectural motifs, there are lively landscapes, attributed to Lambert Sustris, a Flemish artist who collaborated with Titian.

The most interesting room in the villa is the so-called *stanza degli dei*, with figures in ancient garb alternating with landscapes and aedicules framed by painted, faux marble pilasters.

In 1567 further work was undertaken

at the behest of the new bishop Luigi Pisani. This work was directed by Andrea da Valle, an architect and stonemason from Valle di Capodistria, *proto* of the Padua and Santa Giustina Duomos.

He not only restored the building, but also enclosed the large western courtyard within a wall with three large entrance gates. He also directed work on the addition to the terrace overlooking the courtyard, which led to the completion in 1579 of a five-

Opposite page: remains of 16th-century decorations attributed to the Flemish artist Lambert Sustris in the current dining room.

Below: details of the so-called Stanza degli Dei, by Lambert Sustris, with figures in ancient garb.

arch loggia appended to the western front of the podium. The complex, inspired by the "modern method", despite the majesty of its intertwining staircases and the courtyard walls punctuated by stone crescent moons and spheres, did not influence the Veneto architecture of the period, and remained an isolated example.

The agricultural buildings are enclosed within a rustic courtyard alongside the seigneurial courtyard. The complex now belongs to the Olcese family, who have undertaken much restoration and maintenance on the buildings.

Below: the middle room, with evident 18th-century additions to the stucco decorations.

Opposite page: detail of bath room after restoration work undertaken in the 20th century.

Villa Garzoni

Pontecasale

Entrance to rustic courtyard, Villa Garzoni.

Opposite page: large enclosing wall, Villa Pontecasale.

Nadal de Garzoni, a Venetian citizen, listed the Pontecasale property in his tithe declaration for 1518. The property was in the rural Paduan district, and was described as a home with courtyard and cultivatable land made up of eight fields and grazing land, specifying that the entire lot had once belonged to Count Alvise dal Verme. Dal Verme, who fought with Filippo Maria Visconti in the fourth war against the Venetians, had had all his land confiscated after the Cremona Peace Treaty in 1441.

The patrician Bernardo Zane had then bought the land when it was auctioned off, which he almost immediately sold to the Malvezzi counts of Bologna, who in their turn sold the land to the Garzoni family, who then bought up surrounding land in 1455, 1462 and 1465. The Garzonis, originally from Bologna, had moved to Venice in the late-13th century, and split into two family branches. One branch was co-opted into the Venetian nobility in 1381 after the war against Chioggia (the thirty families who had contributed most to the war effort against Genoa were rewarded by the Maggior Consiglio with noble titles).

It is however the non-noble branch which obtained Venetian citizenship in 1355, thus demonstrating their greater entrepreneurial spirit – they founded a bank in Venice in 1430 and actively took charge of the Pontecasale property, where they reorganised the plots of land into agricultural and arable land and began impressive reclamation and drainage work which was to last decades.

When their bank failed in 1498, the Garzonis, officially *cittadini*, concentrated their efforts on the Pontecasale estate. In 1528 it was inherited by the brothers Nadal, Alvise and Girolamo, who decided to abandon the old home and have it replaced by a very different construction. Thus, in 1539, work began on a new villa. It would be completed some thirty years later.

The *eccellentissimi* Garzoni brothers turned to the most important architect then working in Venice: the Florentine Jacopo Tatti, called Il Sansovino because he had been Andrea Sansovino's (as well as Giuliano da Sangallo's) pupil. After a lengthy stay in Rome and the Sack of Rome (1527), Sansovino had moved to Venice, where he was nominated

Portico and loggia in the middle section of main façade, villa Garzoni.

proto for the *Procuratorie de Supra*, that is the most important governmental offices on the upper floor of the building overlooking St Mark's Square. Completion of the Procuratie Vecchie, the Libreria Marciana, the Campanile Loggetta, the Zecca, the façade for the church of San Geminiano which closed off the *piazza* and was demolished during the 19th-century reorganisation and the idea for the Procuratie Nuove are all due to the restructuring of the site for which Sansovino was called upon. The St Mark Procurators, Giovanni Dolfin and Jacopo Cornaro, also requested his services for their Grand Canal *palazzi*.

From 1532, Sansovino was also the *proto* for the Scuola della Misericordia, where the Garzonis had been ecclesiastical brothers for generations. This is where the commissioners and architect probably met; the end result would be the new Pontecasale villa, where the latest trends in architecture, brought in from Florence and Rome, were to triumph. It was in Florence that Sansovino saw the Medicean Poggio Villa; and in Rome Raffaello's admirable productions. The villa's façade has a wide cordoned ramp, preceded by a group of sculptures. This leads to the entrance portico, which is the real reception hall, and which hides the high podium on which the two *piani signorili* are

constituted by the double order of five arches divided by Doric semicolumns on the ground floor and the Ionic order on the upper floor. The Veneto tradition of the villa with portico and loggia is respected, but completely re-interpreted by Sansovino. Here he adopted a classical lexis with an accentuated horizontal rhythm given to the façade, and conferred by the trabeations delimiting the two floors. This same trabeation continues in part along the sides, along with the repeated string-courses. Along with the central loggia, there is a hanging courtyard which characterises the building and divides it into two symmetrical apartments which open up to the right and left of the portico-loggia, according to a plan inspired by the model of the Greek house as established by Vitruvius and brought back by architectural treatises in the 15th century.

The portico with terrace enclosed by balustrade is extremely impressive. It is held aloft by a wealth of 18th-century statues, which also surround the hanging courtyard along with Doric semicolumns. In the courtyard there are an admirable octagonal well-head, with its balustrades interspersed with foliate shelves, and a complex polychrome flooring divided into four squares. There is also a considerably ingenious series of hydraulic links that collect and provide rain water collected by the roof drains. The water is collected in a cistern under the courtyard. The timbre of the internal rooms is majestic. This is particularly true for the open vestibule and the two side rooms, which constitute a plan which is repeated on

Opposite page. Terraced garden,
Villa Garzoni, with octagonal well-head
and complex polychrome paving.

Wide-angle view of main façade.

constitute a plan which is repeated on the *piano nobile*. On the ground floor, however, there are pavilion vaults that present a structure of extremely decorative circles and ovals, which harks back directly to the Marciana. Equally sublime are the fireplaces in the villa rooms. Perhaps the most noteworthy is the fireplace held aloft by canephorae in the eastern ground-floor room. Sansovino's name has been inscribed on the pedestals.

The villa is preceded by an enclosed rectangular garden subdivided into four areas. The garden is about 100 metres wide and 70 deep, while the seigneurial block is a repetition of the same rectangular form of exactly half the size. The area is delimited to the south by a perspective surrounded by 18th-century statues and to the north by a line of cypress trees. All the other greenery has been introduced recently, and is redolent of the informal garden style. The seigneurial residence is flanked to the east by imposing porticoed brick

barchesse forming an "L" shape. The eastern part of the old farmyard is counterbalanced by a large enclosed pasture to the west.

The architectural details of the *barchesse* suggest not only that they were built in two different periods, but also that they were built later than the Sansovian villa itself. They were probably built after the enclosing walls and their imposing entrance gates, perhaps based on a project by Andrea da Valle, who in that period was *proto* at Santa Giustina in Padua and had been asked by Alvise Garzoni to rebuild the Pontecasale parish church in 1573. In the late 16th century, after the death of Vincenzo Garzoni, the last of the "city" line of the family, the Pontecasale land was divided between the Marcantonio Michiel patricians of the Santi Apostoli line, who received the Sansovino villa, and Andrea Renier, who built a residence in the land surrounding the villa.

Michiel was therefore responsible for building the seigneurial chapel, for the now badly deteriorated Galimberti decorations (circa 1780) in one of the downstairs rooms depicting stories from the life of Doge Domenico Michiel, and for the three busts of various Doges and cardinal Michiel in the ground floor portico-vestibule.

Pontecasale was then inherited by the Martinengo counts and thereafter by the Donà dalle Rose family, who in the 1930s got rid of the original furnishings, including the bronze busts of Victoria and Ammannati and the furniture that Sansovino most probably designed. The complex has belonged to the Carrattero family (Padua) since 1950.

Pensile terrace with balustrade
with 18th-century statuary.

Villa Godi
Malinverni

Lonedo

Aerial view of villa Godi (below) and Villa Piovene (above), with complex of gardens and extraordinary setting.

Opposite page. 16th-century shrine with niche containing modern statue, upper gardens, Villa Godi. In background, view of nearby Villa Piovene.

"In Lonedo, in the Vicenza district, there is the following building belonging to Signor Girolamo de' Godi, placed atop a hill with an awe-inspiring view, and a river which provides for fishing." This is how Palladio begins his description of the Lonedo Villa in his *Four Books on Architecture*, published in Venice in 1570.

The turning point for Andrea di Pietro della Gondola came in 1538, when he met Gian Giorgio Trissino, a member of one of the city's oldest families (boasting French descent, what's more) and famous literary figure who had once been a diplomat in the Papal Court. They met during restoration and embellishing work, closely supervised by the owner himself, on Trissino's villa in Crìcoli, just outside Vicenza in Via Marostegana. Palladio was thirty, showed great potential, but had yet to become successful – in fact, his workshop had closed, forcing him to go back to stonemasonry for Giovanni da Pedemuro, where he had done his apprenticeship. Trissino clearly detected Palladio's genius, and introduced him to the classics

Previous page: severe main façade, Villa Godi, with characteristic central loggia.

Left: terraced garden behind the villa, with remains of citrus garden.

Below: detail of servants' quarters alongside entrance gate, with two 16th-century statues attributed to Girolamo Albanese.

Below: detail of tower and terraced gardens behind the villa, surrounded by thick greenery of 19th-century park.

and introduced him to relatives and friends. One of these was Cavalier Girolamo Godi, who asked Palladio, in about 1540, to draw up a project for a country residence in Lonido, in an amenable spot facing onto Valle dell'Astico (it is difficult to imagine how pretty it must have been, as it has now almost been choked by a plethora of buildings).

The Villa's main front is formed by two compact blocks which jut out just slightly from the central aspect which is opened up by a loggia with three barrel-vaults, which in turn is introduced by a single-ramp flight of steps. The windows punctuate the vast surface of the walls according to a pattern that leaves no room for decorative elements.

The window surrounds are flat, and the Godi family's coat-of-arms and commemorative inscription are the only elements that break with the intentional severity and composure of Palladio's architectural language.

The villa seems to communicate a spiritual attitude that was quite common for the period within Vicenza society, where a growing sense of disquiet led to the heterodox propaganda of the *riformati*.

Even the back façade, with its central jutting body defined by a large Serliana window and two smoke

stacks topped by high chimneys, is perfectly in keeping with the rest of the building. On the other hand, the Lonedo Villa constitutes Palladio's work before his first study trips to Rome and the rest of Italy, where he would finally develop his sense of classical architecture as well as that of Raffaello, Bramante, Baldassare Peruzzi and Giulio Romano. The layout of this "villa house" seems to hark back to the 15th-century model of villa with portico and loggia contained within *torreselle*, or towers.

The interior of the *piano nobile* is surprising for its wealth of pictorial decoration, with perspectival *trompe-*

Opposite page: loggia, Villa Godi, with grotesque decorations, by Gualtiero Padovano.

Left: detail of fresco decorations in the loggia, showing satyr's head, by Gualtiero Padovano; 16th-century fireplace in the Sala di Venere, with fresco of Venus in Vulcan's Furnace, by Giovan Battista Zelotti.

Opposite page: detail of frescoed decorations in the villa's main hall, where Giovan Battista Zelotti created a complex architectural weave framing a battle scene. In the faux window (right) is a seated gentleman, while in the background of the landscape there is a scene depicting the rape of Ganymede.

Below: details of frescoes by Gualtiero Padovano in the so-called Sala dei Cesari.

l'oeils that are in sharp contrast with the spatial rigour of the wall structure. The decorative work in the *piano nobile*, undertaken by three important artists of the period, began with the loggias and the building's right wing in 1552-1553, ten years after Palladio had completed the building. The frescoes are by Gualtiero Padovano, who had learnt his trade under Alvise Cornaro. A few years later, the Godis brought in Giovan Battista Zelotti (from Antonio Badile's workshop, where Paolo Veronese had also worked) to provide paintings for the large hall, the three rooms to the left, the *sala delle stagioni* and the ceiling in the *sala dei trionfi*.

Another Veronese artist, Battista del Moro, one of Francesco Torbido's students and his son-in-law, is responsible for the *sala delle muse e dei poeti*.

The Barchessa, dated 1533 and therefore preceding the villa itself, is also part of the Lonedo complex, as well as the garden (17th- and 18th-century statues by Orazio Marinali) and the Romantic park by Antonio Caregaro Negrin (1852).

The large hall of the guest house now holds the collection of 19th-century Italian paintings belonging to the Malinverni family, who have owned the villa since 1954.

The spatial continuity between Villa Godi and the nearby Villa Piovene (which is also 16th-century and clearly Palladian) is sublime. This continuity was admirably filmed by Visconti, who used Villa Godi as the country home of the Serpieri family in *Senso* (1954).

Villa Pisani

Bagnolo

Aerial view of the villa, highlighting relationship with river.

Opposite page. Detail of façade giving on to the river, with rusticated loggia surmounted by tympanum flanked by two towers.

With the law passed by the Veneto Senate on June 30, 1520, all towers and fortresses on the mainland, along with the land they were built on, were expropriated by the *Rason Vecchie*. This is how the Venetians got back at those who sided with Maximilian and the Imperial forces during the Cambrai League. One such "turncoat" was Girolamo Nogarola, whose family had been given its Bagnolo land by the Scaligeris along with the feudal rights associated with the title of Count, conceded in 1387 by the emperor Wenceslaus. In 1523, the Bagnolo fief and its title were bought by N H Giovanni Pisani of the Santo Stefano branch, known as *The Bankers* because of the family's credit business. The amount paid was 13,002 ducats for the 1,200 fields plus various adjuncts and the Nogarola tower over the Guà river.

In 1539 the Pisanis began a series of imposing reclamation and drainage works and introduced rice cultivation on a vast scale.

The Nogarola tower, damaged during the war, was demolished and the magnificent sirs the Counts Vittorio,

Marco and Daniele, the Pisani brothers, decided to construct a building in keeping with the administration of the large amount of land and the family's elevated patrician rank. This was in the early 1640s, when Andrea di Pietro della Gondola, i.e. Palladio, was finishing off Villa Godi in Lonedo and had just got back from his first study trip to Rome with Gian Giorgio Trissino. This was the first building he undertook for a powerful Venetian family with great influence and almost limitless financial means at their disposal. For the Pisanis, who were patrician by birth and had bought the count title, he devised a villa which brought together the prestige of the feudal castle (symbolically referred to by the two towered bodies flanking the main façade, which in turn faces on to the Guà river) and the magniloquence of fashionable Roman architecture (represented by the design and proportion of the loggia that introduces the majestic cruciform central staircase). The loggia is made up of three large arched windows held up by pilasters. The decorations, paired rusticated conches with Ionic lesenes on the sides and single in the central fascia, are finished off by the classical frieze of the architrave, on top of which is positioned the triangular fronton with its central family coat-of-arms with rampant lion surmounted by heraldic crest. Entrance to the loggia is via a semi-circular flight of steps which corresponds to the central arch, while the side arches are closed off with a stone balustrade with small pilasters. According to the design published in the 1570 treatise, the façade facing onto the family's land, simple and compact in the articulation of the openings along the surface and where the only original note is constituted by the large central thermal window, there was to be a jutting hexastyle pronaos with triangular fronton, a central and two lateral staircases. The building was also supposed to be closed off by two wings of barchesse forming a quadri-portico. The Pisanis, however, opted for a detached warehouse and servants' quarters. They were particularly proud of their farmyard, which was exactly the same size as St Mark's Square. Unfortunately these

Previous page: unfinished façade giving on to the countryside, with characteristic central thermal window.

Opposite page: the long arm of the central cruciform hall with barrel-vault ceiling. The central section contains a mythological scene.

Left: detail of cross vault in the central hall.

Below: grotesque decorations in the cross vault.

large barchesse were partly damaged during World War II.

The large service building with central portico, to the left of the garden area which opens out in front of the façade giving onto the countryside, was built later. As was the current lateral entrance to the late-Neo-classical courtyard. In fact the channelling of the Guà river and ensuing embankments compromised the original relationship between villa and river.

The interior layout of the villa is consonant with the tradition Venetian plan with symmetrically organised side rooms coming off the central hall covered with a cross-vault which in its turn contains a barrel vault. The anonymous ceiling frescoes respect contemporary tastes. The cross-vault contains grotesques, while the barrel vault was provided with frescoes representing the myth of Phaethon being aided by nymphs after his fall into the Po. Other anonymous wall paintings can be found in the

Detail of ceiling decorations, ground floor hall, southern tower. In the lower section there are scenes from the Decameron and Orlando Furioso.

ground floor rooms in the southern tower. The subjects are based on the *Decameron* and *Orlando Furioso,* and cover the upper portions of the walls and the pavilion ceiling. There is a very interesting sculpted stone hand basin in the so-called large kitchen. The stairs leading to the mezzanine were altered in the 19th century when the villa was restored and subdivided (the structure was restored to its original form between 1976 and 1993 by the Pisanis' descendants, the Counts Ferri de' Lazara). The villa is now owned by Bedeschi.

Detail of rectangular west room.

Ground-floor room, southern tower, with glimpse of connected rooms.

La Badoera

Fratta Polesine

Fratta, which is situated on slightly higher land, has preserved its original function of river transit point despite the changes to the landscape over the years due to floods, and provides a link between Venice and Ferrara. Territorial impositions brought to bear by the Venetian Republic after 1484, when the Polesine district was taken from the Estensis, led to vast drainage work, the introduction of water pipelines, reclamation of land and ensuing increases in agricultural production.

In 1519, the Venetian state auctioned off a series of plots of land, including the so-called lands of the *Vespara alla Fratta*, to raise money for the Cambrai wars. According to documents, the land was bought by the patrician Giovan Francesco Loredan along with his business partner and father-in-law Giorgio Corner, knight and *procuratore de citra*, i.e. procurator for the area on the St Mark's side of the Grand Canal, as well as candidate for the Doge-ship of Venice and brother to Catherine, Queen of Cyprus. The land was later apportioned out between the two, and the Fratta land went to Giorgio

Loredan, the only male heir to Giovan Francesco. Giorgio died young without heirs and left his property to his two sisters Lucietta, who had married his great friend Francesco Badoer, and Lucrezia, who had married Vincenzo Grimani.

It was Badoer who commissioned Andrea Palladio in 1555 to build a villa on his wife's land. Shortly after, Grimani also decided to build a dominical home which was then bequeathed to his son-in-law Andrea Molin.

Today, Palladio's Villa Badoer and the Molins' villa, which the anonymous architect had ideally intended to be similar to Palladio's, continue to speak to each other and form a unique urban system that provides a characteristic note to the town of Fratta Polesine, which more than others owes its existence to patrician Venetian presence on the mainland.

The Badoera was already built and inhabited by 1556, and became the headquarters for Francesco Badoer's feudal business, including his direction of the reclaiming and drainage of the area's swamp lands. The building's central body, ennobled by a pronaos

Detail of enclosing walls and left servants' quarters, added in the 18th century.

Detail of loggia, with grotesque decorations.

Opposite page: detail of the access flight of steps with the conjunction of the right barchessa.

with six Ionic columns holding up the architrave which in its turn holds aloft the large triangular tympanum, is crowned by two curvilinear rustic side wings with Tuscan columns. These were Palladio's first exedra barchesse, which he would later adopt for other projects such as the Trissino villa in Meledo (where, however, they got no further than the planning stage).

The front staircase leading up to the loggia (of exactly the same width) is punctuated by three broad ramps, and is mainly responsible for the majesty of the villa as a whole. The ground-floor podium, which is five feet high (as Palladio himself wrote in his *Four Books*), holds up the entire parallelepiped volume of the villa and housed the suggestive servants' quarters. The *piano nobile* is hierarchically evident thanks to its elevated position, chosen to keep flood waters at bay. Above this there are the granaries. The simplicity of the decorative elements, with frameless windows deprived of all decoration, is also evident in the back façade which is embellished by a simple dentilled cornice and string-course above the ground floor windows. This façade, in fact, has no pronaos, even though the original plan was to include a jutting pronaos with external staircase.

The Badoera is surrounded by walls with a characteristic motif of small upturned arches similar to the one Sansovino had used for Villa Pontecasale; here, however, the arches are embellished by a series of white stone spheres. The bridge, built shortly after 1556 over Canale Scortico in front of the villa, helps underscore the specific axial criteria according to which Palladio planned the building, even though subsequent embankments have compromised the original relationship between the villa and the watercourse.

Previous page: Badoera façade, with majestic hexastyle loggia.

Opposite page: complex grotesque decorations by Giallo Fiorentino in one of the lateral rooms.

Above: detail of loggia decorations with a member of the Compagnia della Calza inviting guests to enter.

Center: the central hall of the villa, with decorations by Giallo Fiorentino rediscovered during restoration work in the 1960s.

Belove: detail of the decoration in a side room, with Pegasus taking flight.

Giuseppe Gaetano Badoer died, heirless, in 1678. In 1681, Badoer's sisters partitioned his property, and the Fratta lands and buildings went to Paolina, Marcantonio Mocenigo's wife. It was therefore this family who transformed the granaries into domestic quarters, had the ceilings lowered in the master apartment (vaults were introduced to hide the original beams), had the baroque Mocenigo family coat-of-arms placed in the middle of the tympanum instead of the Badoer coat-of-arms, had the two barchesse extended in about 1780 and had the two twin fountains installed in the garden in front of the villa. Further changes were made in the early 19th century when the villa was bequeathed to the Del Vecchio family. The villa was bought by the then Ente per le Ville Venete in the 1960s, who then proceeded to undertake restoration work and demolished the interior superfetations. Even though not quite whole, it was during this restoration that the original frescoes were found (they had been plastered as early as 1676).

The loggia and the interior of the villa were frescoed by Giallo Fiorentino, a Tuscan painter belonging to the Salviati circle, who was cited by Palladio himself as a famous author of grotesques. Giallo Fiorentino also painted the fresco cycle in the hall and side rooms of the adjacent Villa Grimani Molin. But if the dominant theme in Villa Molin is the feats of the Molin family, the frescoes in the Badoera are much more difficult to interpret. We should perhaps go back to Francesco Badoer and Giorgio Loredan, his friend and brother-in-law, owner of the Fratta plot of land. Along with twelve other young Venetians, they had both given life to the *Compagnia della Calza degli Accessi*, a theatrical production company. This is what the grotesques in the loggia seem to allude to with the two "compagni della calza" inviting visitors to enter the villa. The mythological episodes in the central hall, framed by grotesques, are instead a celebration of the reclamations promoted by the Badoers, while the intertwined coats-of-arms of the Badoers and Loredans are testimony to the alliance between the two houses. The villa is now owned by the Rovigo Provincial Council.

Villa Barbaro
Masèr

In 1550, on the death of Francesco Barbaro, who belonged to an illustrious patrician family, the Treviso lands of Masèr with villa on the slopes of a small wooded hill, with frescoes that had only just been completed by Giovan Battisti Ponchini and Girolamo Mazzoni some two years earlier, was bequeathed to his sons Daniele and Marcantonio. Daniele, who had graduated from Padua, after having been ambassador to England, was nominated coadjutor of the Patriarch of Aquileia Giovanni Grimani, with the title of Patriarch Elect. In 1552-3 he represented the Venetian Senate at the Council of Trent. Marcantonio's was an even more brilliant career. He served the Republic, first as ambassador to France at the court of Catherine de' Medici, regent on behalf of her son Charles IX, and then to Turkey at the court of the Grand Visir, just before the Battle of Lepanto. On his return, the Council of Ten nominated him Procurator *de supra*, the second-highest office in Venice, that is superintendent of the Basilica.

Both humanist scholars, Daniele published a commented edition of Vitruvius' ten books on architecture, while Marcantonio specialised in sculpture.

Palladio therefore had to deal with two consummate patricians, with whom he was also friends.

In 1554, when Palladio and Daniele Barbaro had just got back from a trip to Rome, work began on the new Masèr villa, which absorbed the previous building. The building was completed in 1558, albeit not without anomalies.

The layout included two porticoed

barchesse, closed off by two towers, flanking the main house. But the dominical block jutted out a lot more along the sides, giving the complex an unusual "T" shape. The central cruciform hall, followed by the *sala dell'Olimpo* in the part of the villa looking out towards the nymphaeum, lost its function as the only fulcrum in the noble apartment. Even the façade without pronaos is atypical for Palladio, just as are the barchesse, which are only slightly higher than the central building, and the two side buildings which with their august façades vie with the main building,

throwing off balance the hierarchy between the seigneurial building and its adjacent structures – extremely rare in Palladio's works. The route to the reception halls, what's more, is not by means of a ground floor entrance in the central body, but rather by way of lateral staircases that are reached via the porticoes. These and other elements have led to the conclusion that Daniele Barbaro had a hand in planning the villa, which on the one hand seems to be inspired by ancient residences, and on the other by contemporary Roman architecture,

Overall view and detail of large cruciform lobby in southern wing. The frescoed walls, by Paolo Veronese, contain architectural motifs with landscapes along the longer arms and niches with playing figures along the shorter arms. The vault, now white, was originally decorated with vine-shoot and floral motifs.

and especially Villa Madama, which Raffaello had begun and Antonio da Sangallo the Younger had completed. The themes can even be seen in the secret garden behind the villa and in the nymphaeum which communicates directly with the *piano nobile*. Here the tautologous decorations and a certain ingenuity in the sculptures seem to lead directly to Marcantonio Barbaro and his amateur love for sculpture. The Barbaro brothers commissioned the cycle of frescoes painted between 1560 and 1566 by Paolo Veronese, who is not cited by Palladio in his

treatise, perhaps because he had been put off by the grandeur of the pictorial decorations which sometimes overwhelm the clean, balanced spaces of the architecture.

The iconography was probably dictated by Daniele Barbaro, who wanted to celebrate the theme of the family's harmony and peace, alluding to his close relationship with his brother, and of the state, considering that both brothers held office in the highest echelons of the Republic's magistrature.

Detail of the so-called Stanza dell'Olimpo, where Giustiniana Giustinian, owner and wife of Marcantonio Barbaro, and a wet nurse can be seen looking out from a gallery.

Opposite page. Row of rooms, Villa Barbaro, with a **trompe-l'oeil** *containing a supposed self-portrait by Paolo Veronese.*

This is what the eight players in the cruciform hall and the *sala dell'Olimpo* seem to allude to; while the celestial representation in the vault contains those deities who, by being transformed into planets, are also part of the Christian cosmos. There are observers of this Olympian congregation: Giustiniana Giustinian, Marcantonio's wife, with wet nurse and the two children Francesco and Almorò. The frescoes continue in the other rooms, among stuccos and fireplaces attributed to Alessandro Vittoria, landscapes between faux columns and *trompe-l'oeils* of characters facing out of doorways (tradition has it that one of these is Paolo Veronese himself).

On the road in front of the main entrance to the villa there is a fountain of Neptune, just beyond which there is a small temple which Marcantonio had built in 1580 as the town church, where Palladio re-elaborated the Roman pantheon with a hexastyle pronaos with imaginative stucco festoons, and with an articulated cylindrical body holding aloft a cupola crowned by a lantern and flanked by two small twin campanili. The later external sculptures are by Orazio Marinali, while there are works by Alessandro Vittoria inside. The Masèr church was Palladio's last work; he died the year it was built. Villa Barbaro was then handed down to the patrician families of the Trevisans, the Bassadonnas and then the Manins. The complex was bought by the Friuli industrialists the Giacomellis in 1840. This latter family might have been responsible for the characteristic yellow colour of the exterior of the villa, which was sold to Count Giuseppe Volpi di Misurata in 1934. His descendents are the current owners of the villa.

Count Volpi undertook restoration work which took longer than anticipated. This touched on both the interior, where the Russian Nicola Lochoff worked on the décor, and the exterior, and particularly on the gardens which were redesigned by Tomaso Buzzi, an architect from Sondrio. Buzzi modified the road leading up to the villa by reorganising the space in front of the main building and eliminating the 18th-century statues of putti, which were moved to the little rose garden under the left tower. This garden was given a chequered form, where grass alternated with paving. Buzzi also worked on the secret garden opposite the radically redesigned nymphaeum according to a geometric plan of lines and surfaces where the grassy, stone and paving elements are counterposed, thus providing one of the rare examples of a rationalist garden.

Villa Emo

Fanzolo

Wide-angle view of main façade,
Villa Emo.

Opposite page: detail of middle section,
with fronton with two winged Victories
holding aloft the Emo coat-of-arms.

For the villa in Fanzolo, in the Treviso plain, Palladio chose a plan including barchesse aligned with the seigneurial body, imposing the porticos on simple masonry pilasters; the columns, a noble architectural element, were reserved for the main residence. Beyond the enclosure there are rows of workers' houses, forming a small rural village depending on the villa.

Perhaps the architect and the commissioner, the patrician Leonardo Emo, were influenced in their choice of the overall layout (which is similar to that of Villa Masèr) by the very famous nearby villa that Alvise Soranzo had built, in about 1540, in Treville (Castelfranco Veneto), by the Verona architect Michele Sanmicheli. Unfortunately all that remains of this villa is part of one of the barchesse, after the demolition undertaken in 1817, and descriptions, including one by Vasari, pictorial representations of the villa before it was demolished and fragments of the frescoes, now in various collections, of a cycle by Paolo Veronese.

Leonardo Emo, born in 1473 to a "new family" included among the patrician families of Venice by the Maggior

*Opposite page: perspectival view
of one of the two porticos flanking
the main body.*

*Below: details of sculptural decorations in
the Italian garden, Villa Emo.*

Consiglio, had shown considerable political and military talent during the Cambrai War. After his victory over French troops in Brescia in 1509, he was one of the main players in the defence of Padua from the Imperial army of Maximilian I. After becoming senator, Leonardo, who was perfectly placed to aspire to the highest office of the state, was defeated by Pietro Lando and then Andrea Gritti in his two runs for the doge-ship. But Leonardo also dedicated lots of his time to looking after the land he had bought in Fanzolo from the Barbarigo family. He managed to get

water to this land in 1536, when he brought his mainland ingenuity to bear and obtained a tract of water, the so-called Barbarigo *seriola*, which was an offshoot of Brentella Canal. He was also one of the first to cultivate corn, which had just recently been introduced from the Americas.

Leonardo passed away in 1559 at the age of 86, more or less when Palladio was building the villa. His heir was his nephew and namesake Leonardo Emo, who, in the general Castelfranco assessment of 1561, declared a villa, *barchesse*, *colombare*, citrus gardens and

Opposite page. Central hall, with frescoes by Giovan Battista Zelotti.
In the middle section there is the episode of the murder of Virginia.

Below: detail of the frescoes in the central hall, showing the magnanimity of Scipio, thus exalting the virtue and chastity of the Ancients;
center: general view of the central hall, with magniloquent faux-architectural decorations;
right: the heraldic coat-of-arms of the Emo family above the Lion of St Mark.

land – from which it can be assumed that the complex was well under way at that stage.

In this complex, the simplicity of Palladio's lines serves to exalt the harmony of the proportions, with a main square block (about 27x27 metres), placed over a ground floor servants' quarters and flanked by two long barchesse with eleven arches, closed off by towers.

Four giant Doric columns ennoble the pronaos running along the façade, which is reached via a majestic staircase. These columns hold up the evident trabeation which holds up the triangular fronton, in the centre of which there is the Emo family coat-of-arms held aloft by angels (by Alessandro Vittoria).

This Fanzolo complex is therefore nothing if not functional, able to satisfy the productive needs of a farm; but at the same time it is also monumental, a representation of patrician dignity on the mainland.

Palladio resolved the relationship between villa and landscape with rare

Left: detail of Painting in the Sala delle Arti..

Opposite page: detail of decoration, Autumn, over door in the Sala delle Arti.

*Page 144: **stanza delle Arti**, allegory depicting Astronomy and Poetry.*

Page 145: detail of grotesque decoration in one of the small rooms.

mastery. He provides two axes at right angles with one another, which are the villa and its adjuncts on the one hand and the 1.4 km drive to the complex, which precedes then follows the complex and coincides with the orthogonal fulcrum of Via Postumia. Unfortunately, this original layout has been replaced by the diagonally structured modern roads and railroad. The interior (the original ceilings and skylights conceived by Palladio for the vestibule and main hall were restored between 1937 and 1940) contains a remarkable fresco cycle painted by Giovan Battista Zelotti in about 1565, most probably on the occasion of the young Leonardo's marriage with Cornelia Grimani.

On the loggia walls can be found paintings representing mythological figures, as well as a representation of Ceres, the goddess of agriculture. In the hall the allegories of Cordiality and Economy lead to the central hall with painted Corynthian columns which divide the walls into areas where, in the central area, there are representations of the Death of Virginia and Scipio the African freeing a Carthaginian princess from slavery

(an example of the virtue and chastity of the ancients); the lateral frames contain Cibele, Neptune, Juno and Jove as representations of the four elements. Prudence and Abundance can be found in the tympanum over the entrance. This iconographic structure is an obvious allusion to the magnanimity and industry of the commissioners.

In the rooms respectively dedicated to Venus, Hercules and Io there are mainly mythological subjects which provide ample compositions with landscapes, while the *sala delle Arti* is dominated by female figures. The

grotesques decorating the small lateral rooms are also noteworthy.

Towards the second half of the 19th century, the Vicenza architect Antonio Caregaro Negrin was brought in to transform the front garden with the introduction of evergreens and the area along the right hand side of the villa, where a woods was created according to the current interest for informal gardens.

Villa Emo is the only Palladian villa that still belongs to the family which originally commissioned the villa.

La Rotonda

Vicenza

Aerial view of the villa.

Opposite page: the Rotonda seen from the Bacchiglione.

In 1570, Palladio published his *Four Books on Architecture*, a treatise which is exemplary for its clarity and humanity as well as its drawings and illustrations. La Rotonda is included in volume two, among the city buildings and not the villas. Particularly significant is the fact that no mention is made of the economic aspects relating to agriculture that characterise the building, which is Palladio's most famous and imitated building through the ages. The exclusion of La Rotonda from the category of villa-farms, despite the enormous quantity of land possessed by the commissioner Paolo Almerico in the region (so vast, in fact, that it had to be subdivided into an elaborate series of farmlands), further underlines the intellectual choices made by both the owner and the architect.

The site itself is fundamental, and is amply commented on by Palladio in his treatise: "amenable and delightful: because it is upon a little hill which can be very easily climbed and is watered along one side by the navigable Bacchiglione and on the other it is surrounded by other amenable hills that give the impression of a very large theatre, and all the fields are cultivated and abound in the most excellent and tasty fruits and excellent grapevines: hence it enjoys from all quarters most beautiful views, some of which are foreshortened, others much longer, and others yet are limited only by the Horizon".

La Rotonda was thus built so as to enhance the area's natural and almost limitless views. The layout is of the central type, based on the shape of a square in the centre of which there is a circular space which is reached from the outside by way of four short passageways, structured according to

two different orthogonal symmetries denotated by the different size of the corridors and the layout of the lateral rectangular rooms. The exterior gives us four identical scores in the four façades, which are framed by jutting Ionic pronaos preceded by staircases enclosed by high walls. The equilibrium between the sacred character of the temple and the domestic dimension of the house is what characterises the building.

The presence of such a marked symbolic dimension may well have found in Palladio the perfect architect, but the commissioner, and especially his character, are equally responsible for the final outcome.

Paolo Almerico was born in Vicenza in 1514 to a noble family, even though it was not included among the great families of the city. At the age of 14 he obtained a prebend for the city's cathedral provided by Clement VII. He then moved to Padua to study arts and canonical law. Here he became embroiled in a case of homicide, which led to two years' imprisonment even though he was later fully acquitted. He subsequently travelled to Rome, where he was an apostolic referendary for Pius IV and Pius V. In 1567 he returned to Vicenza, where he decided to begin work on La Rotonda.

The fact that he sold his ancestral home in Pozzo Rosso and moved to a provisional home in Ponzano when the Palladian villa was begun give us some measure of how much Paolo wanted to see the Rotonda completed.

By 1570, building had reached the roof stage, even though it is not clear whether the current cupola belongs to this period. Palladio died in 1580; Paolo Almerico in 1589. In 1591 Almerico's heir, an illegitimate son called Almerigo, sold the property to Counts Odorico and Mario Capra of the branch known as Strà Grande (currently Corso Palladio), where their city houses were to be found.

Odorico, an important figure in the Vicenza of his time, held several public offices. Mario, on the other hand, was slightly more retiring, and spent his time looking after the family's possessions, including the building known as La Rotonda. The Capras paid 18,500 ducats for the property, and 12,126 were then spent on work undertaken, at least in part, by Vincenzo Scamozzi. It is probably Scamozzi who is responsible for the stepped cupola which is clearly lower than the drawing provided by Palladio, even though it is difficult to determine whether this was Scamozzi's doing or Palladio who had changed his mind. What is certain is that the lantern on top of the cupola dates from after the Capras' purchase, along with the acroterial statues by Giambattista Albanese, and the pictorial and stucco decorations in some of the interior rooms. These decorations were undertaken in two different periods: the first in about 1600 by Alessandro Maganza, who decorated the inside of the cupola; the second about a century later when the French painter Lodovico Dorigny provided painted scenes for the living room walls and stucco artists provided the baroque decorations over the door-jambs.

Between 1725 and 1740, Francesco Muttoni from Porlezza provided the residential features in the attic, which was originally a single undivided space, and the mezzanines when the internal wooden spiral staircases were added.

From the period of Almerico and Palladio, however, date the frescoes in the corner rooms, the grotesques in the small rooms, Lorenzo Rubini's statues along the spurs of the staircases, the stuccoes on the ceilings and the fireplace tassels (considering the amount of work involved, this was undertaken by several moulders and shapers from the circle of Alessandro Vittoria, one of the most popular sculptors of the period).

The adjacent and less obvious rustic buildings built by the Capra family were probably the work of Vincenzo Scamozzi, while the seigneurial chapel, designed by Girolamo Albanese, was built between 1645 and 1663.

The Rotonda, after having belonged to the Capra family until the early 19th century, eventually went to the Valmarana counts of the Venetian branch of the family, who have kept it in perfect condition.

Left: detail of the frescoes on the ceiling in a side passage.

Opposite page: the cupola over the round room with frescoes by Alessandro Maganza and the superabundant baroque decorations.

Villa della Torre

Fumane

Above: façade facing on to the valley, Villa della Torre, with double flight of steps leading to the terraced garden.

Opposite page: the bridge over the fish ponds opposite the façade facing on to the valley.

One of the branches of the powerful Milanese della Torre family, arch enemies of the Viscontis during the power struggle for control over Milan, arrived in Verona in the first half of the 14th century. One of the members of the Torre di San Fermo branch, from the parish where they lived, was Giulio, a man of letters and amateur collector of antiques and medals. In 1504 he married Anna, the sole heir to Guido Antonio Maffei, owner of houses in Contrada Sant'Egidio, where they eventually moved, and a vast tithe

in Fumane in Valpolicella. On the death of his father-in-law in 1520, Giulio inherited the Fumane land and houses, to which he added further land purchased in 1533-1534.

It is most probably thanks to Giulio della Torre that the old Maffei *palazzo* was restored.

Besides Giulio, however, we should also mention his two sons, Girolamo and Francesco, both of whom were part of the Verona Bishopric's retinue (Girolamo was responsible for the cathedral; Francesco was Bishop Matteo Giberti's personal secretary).

Giberti was a cultured, intelligent man, a refined diplomat and a brilliant man of the world. Born in Palermo of Genoese descent, he was datekeeper for Pope Clement VII, and, between 1524 and 1543, he brought to Verona people of the calibre of Pietro Bembo, Giovanni della Casa, Francesco Berni, Matteo Bandello, Girolamo Facastoro and Giulio Romano, whom he commissioned to undertake the cartoons for the frescoes in the apsidal conch of the duomo.

This was the cultural milieu the della Torres frequented, and this is where

we must look if we are to appreciate the restoration work undertaken on the Fumane villa in the late 1650s.

The articulation of the complex is reminiscent of Giulio Romano's work on Palazzo Te, and precisely on the two symmetrical buildings, one of which encapsulates the ancient Maffei palace. These two buildings flank an internal porticoed courtyard, a veritable peristyle, which then opens up towards the garden, which is reached via a small arched bridge spanning a fish pond. Even the use of rough rustication which, from the portals to the pilasters of the peristyle to the bridge arches, is continually found in Villa della Torre, harks back to Pippi architecture. There are also echoes of Veronese architecture, such as the three rusticated arches in the Arena wing, the tufa ornament of Porta Nuova and Porta San Zeno by Sanmicheli, which already existed in the 1540s, and Palazzo Bevilacqua in the Corso, built by 1534 by the same architect.

In fact Sanmicheli and Giulio Romano are often mentioned in connection

Left: peristyle, Villa della Torre.

*Above: the Serlian portico that leads to the
entrance loggia, seigneurial chapel.*

with Villa della Torre, but what excludes this paternity is Pippi's death in 1546, while the villa was built about ten years later.

However, the ingeniousness of the idea, which the villa and Palazzo Te both definitely share, is not matched by the execution itself, which is certainly below the qualitative levels of people of the calibre of Giulio Romano and Sanmicheli.

It is therefore very likely that it was Giulio della Torre and his sons Girolamo and Francesca who came up with the idea of a house which, inspired by Palazzo Te, offers examples of a close study of Vitruvius' writings in the *house of the Ancients*. The della Torres, what's more, extended the attention paid to the main building to the organisation of the space leading up to and beyond the villa, organising within the strip of rectangular land, which delicately slopes up towards the Fumane hill, a succession of five quadrangular floors aligned according to the same axis. The succession is from highest to lowest order, following the natural slope of the land, via brief flights of steps that link the land, once planted with lines of cypress trees, to the entrance courtyard and the residential building, to the fish pond and then to the lower garden. The refined *jeux d'eau*, which are only recognisable in part and use tubs and fountains deployed right up to the nymphaeum below the fish pond, and then the fountain (no longer extant) in the lower garden, are directly linked to the culture that permeates the period's villa architecture within the Roman context, from Pope Julius III's Vigna, Monte all'Acqua Vergine, to Cardinal Ippolito II's villa at Tivoli.

The fulcrum of the composition is the villa itself, while the country houses which are hidden by a high wall can be reached through an entrance gate in the front courtyard, which also contains the seigneurial chapel dedicated to Santa Maria della Corte.

The small temple has an octagonal layout preceded by an oval loggia with a rusticated ashlar Serliana, the design for which has been attributed to Sanmicheli, as Giorgio Vasari reminds us in his *Le vite de più eccellenti pittori, scultori ed architettori* (1568). The year 1558 inscribed in the bronze bell of the campanile, whose crenellated crown alludes to the heraldic coat-of-arms of the della Torre family, is the year work was completed on the building.

During restoration work undertaken on the interiors in the 1960s floral motifs dating to the early 15th century and a small altar ascribable to the workshop of the Veronese craftsman Giovanni Badile were discovered. There were also earlier decorations, which date back to an even older building.

In the 16th century were added the articulated and complex ceilings that decorate many of the villa's rooms, as well as the masked monumental fireplaces, which have been attributed to Bartolomeo Ridolfi, which adorn four whole rooms on the ground floor, and which are stylistically closely linked to those in the Palladian Palazzo Thiene in Vicenza.

The strange atmosphere of Villa della Torre has been evoked in the poetry of the Venetian poet and courtesan Veronica Franco, who stayed in the building in 1575 as a guest of the then owner Marcantonio della Torre.

Since the Napoleonic era, the villa has had many owners, with subsequent expropriations and inappropriate uses, culminating with World War II. This contributed to the complex's poor state of repair, which was put right by the Cazzola family from Verona, who have owned the building since 1951.

Il Catajo

Battaglia Terme

The suggestive name of Catajo, which many have felt resonates with the sound of Marco Polo's mythical Cathay, is in fact documented in the late 13th century as *Chataio*, or rather *ca' tajo*, and that is *casa del taglio* or "the house of excavation". Considering the morphology of the area, among the foothills of Montenuovo, at the feet of the Colli Euganei, and Canale di Battaglia, it is not difficult to imagine work being undertaken on the embankments or for the foundations of buildings. In fact, as early as the 15th century there are descriptions of a house with courtyard, farmland and aviary, owned by the Obizzi family in the act of division between Giovan Pietro and his uncle Girolamo Obizzi. According to the family tree, the family arrived in Italy from Burgundy in the wake of Henry II of Saxony, the Roman emperor and king of Germany. Once they settled in Lucca, the Obizzis began to have links with the city of Padua as early as 1285, when a certain Guglielmo Malaspina Obizzi arrived as *podestà*. In fact it was in 1422 that the Obizzi family took up permanent residency in Padua when Antonio from Ferrara,

Opposite page: nymphaea in the large fish pond in the garden towards the valley.

Above: aerial view of the magnificent Catajo complex, including the long buildings used as barracks.

where he had been employed by the Este family, married the rich Paduan heiress Negra de' Negri, who brought with her the Battaglia lands as part of her dowry. It was not until Pio Enea I of the Obizzis, a man of arms for the Serenissima and inventor of a flame thrower, the *obice*, that work began on the current house, built between 1570 and 1573 according to a design put together by Pio Enea himself, probably in collaboration with the then Santa Giusta *proto* in Padua, Andrea da Valle, and paid for with money deriving from the conspicuous dowry of his wife Eleonora Martinengo.

Pio Enea decided to extend the house towards the hill in the early 16th century, with a loggia giving on to the canal and terraced garden, where his mother, Beatrice Pio from Correggio, held a cultured literary salon. Pio Ennea wanted to erect a building that would testify to the family's military origins and particularly his role as leader of a mercenary company. The aspect he therefore underscores for the Catajo, conditioned by the position between hill, canal and driveway, is that of a fortress with battlements, watch towers, drawbridge and high

Page 160: view of southern garden in the old house, which was part of Negra de' Negri's dowry; in the background, Pio Enea's castle.

Page 161: detailed view of the watchtowers and terraces.

Opposite page: view of the **Cortile dei Giganti***, with Pio Enea I's stables, which Pio Enea II transformed into a theatre and armoury.*

Above: the Cortile dei Giganti with the old de' Negri house, the nucleus of Il Catajo.

Below: details of the elephant fountain and the Bacchiglione fountain.

surrounding walls, called *Castelvecchio*. The building contains many and very eloquent citations; what's more, the large surfaces of the façade of the main block contained enormous frescoed scenes of battle, which have since been lost but which the man of letters Giuseppe Betussi talks about in his *Ragionamento sopra Chataio* (1553). Betussi also inspired the celebratory subjects, a mix between historical fact and legend, of the frescoes decorating the rooms along the *piano nobile*, which were undertaken circa 1571-73 by Giovan Battista Zelotti and his workshop. In the main hall and the adjacent rooms there is a chronological succession of forty frames, surrounded by faux architectural motifs, depicting the episodes that make up the history of the Obizzis: from their arrival in Genoa following Henry II of Saxony to the marriage of Negra de' Negri, which marked the beginning of the Paduan branch of the family. Even the apartment on the third floor has interesting fresco decorations, especially in the so-called *camera delle imprese* and in that of the *vedute*, where there are bird's-eye-views of Rome, Florence, Venice and Genoa.

On Pio Enea I's death in 1589, the Catajo was inherited by his officially recognised illegitimate son Roberto, who rarely lived there.

In 1648, confirming his birthright, the Castle of Catajo went to Pio Enea II, another man of arms who had been made marquis of Orciano by Cosimo II of Tuscany. He had so little respect for institutions that he spent four years in jail by order of the Duke of Este, and was later banished from the city of Padua for one year. Pio Enea II degli Obizzi, however, unlike his father Roberto, really loved the Battaglia property,

which he extended and improved by raising the entrance driveway up to the level of the courtyard in front of the building and the creation of a large garden along the canal. Further work, such as the entrance gate transformed into a triumphal arch, was undertaken at the end of the 18th century by Tommaso degli Obizzi, a general for the Duke of Modena, who added his collections of weapons, musical instruments, archaeological finds and coins to the Catajo. Tommaso was also responsible for the reorganisation of the southern garden, with its remarkably large fish pond. In this garden he planted magnolia trees, which had just been introduced from the Americas, instead of the original embroidered *parterre*.

In 1805 Tommaso degli Obizzi died and the Catajo was left to Ercole III d'Este, the Duke of Modena.

Ferdinando IV of Modena and Reggio extended the complex even further. He added a completely new structure, the Castelnuovo, as well as other servants' quarters, and completed the restructuring work on the garden, which was turned into a Romantic park with a large pool. He also had a terraced garden put in between Castelvecchio and Castelnuovo, and called it the *Giardino della Duchessa*.

A series of extensions that were made over the centuries has produced a complex of buildings that are all rigorously at right angles with each other. Courtyards and terraced gardens, loggias and terraces, halls and servants' quarters alternate with each other for a total of 350 rooms, linked by internal and external staircases, corridors and entranceways, some of which excavated from stone, forming a labyrinthine itinerary.

There is an incredible *Cortile dei Giganti*, used by the Obizzis for theatrical shows, and the adjacent *Cortile delle Naumachie*, which could house jousts, tournaments and even naval battles. There are also many fountains (unfortunately no longer in use): the Medoacus Maior, the Brenta river, and the Medoacus Minor, the Bacchiglione, are placed at the entrance; there is a theatrical elephant fountain in a grotto in the *Cortile dei Giganti*, and others dedicated to Cerberus, Janus and Hydra, which contribute to the spectacular wealth of the complex according to an iconographic structure that was in part explained by Francesco Berni in the addendum to the 1669 edition of Betussi's *Ragionamento sopra il Chataio*.

The complex is closed off by an enormous park, known as the *Parco dei Daini*, which extends over Montenovo, where there are still hundreds of specimens of wild deer.

The Dukes of Modena handed the Catajo to the Habsburgs in 1875, who transformed the theatre into a seigneurial chapel dedicated to St Michael and decorated in the German Gothic style. Even though the Habsburgs effectively completed the expropriation of Tommaso degli Obizzi's various collections (which the

Estensis had begun), the Catajo was elected their official summer residence and even hosted the Archduke Ferdinand just a few days before he was assassinated in Sarajevo.

Confiscated during World War I, the Catajo was handed back to the Italian state as part payment for war damages. It was sold to the Dalla Francesca family, the current owners, in 1928.

La Rocca
Pisana

Lonigo

In the early months of 1576, N H Vettor Pisani, co-owner with his brothers Marco and Daniele of the Contea di Bagnolo, which had previously belonged to the Veronese Nogarolas, decided to build a house for pleasure in healthier climate on the hill, the first of the Berici hills which rise to the east of Lonigo.

The Pisanis already had two residential buildings in the area: a villa built by Palladio in about 1542 in Bagnolo along the river Guà, in the midst of enormous rice paddies that provided the family with its great wealth, and a *palazzo* just astride one of the city doors of the walled town of Lonigo.

Vettor's decision to build a house in an isolated part of the country, which was certainly healthier than Bagnolo, came at the same time as the Plague that struck Venice in the late summer of 1575. This is a rather important fact, as recorded by Maccà in his *Storia del territorio vicentino* (1812), where he writes that "during the last Plague" (he is probably referring to the 1630 Plague) "those who survived had all moved to safety at the Rocca, and not a single one died".

What is certain is that Vettor Pisani never saw the Rocca completed, as he

Above: aerial view of the Rocca Pisana, highlighting the cupola with round skylight.

Opposite page: the Rocca Pisana seen from the long entrance drive.

Left: eastern flank and back façade, Rocca Pisana.

Right: view of the façade.

Page 172: the rectangular western staircase with large fireplace with Roman-like tassel.

Page 173: detail of the western spiral staircase; Right: detail of the chapel on the last floor of the villa.

Page 174: above the Serliana in the western wing seen from within; centre: view of the villa's central hall; below: the delicate fretworked grille in the middle of the circular room used to collect rainwater. The grille is directly beneath the cupola skylight.

Page 175: the cupola over the central staircase with a circular fascia punctuated by segmented trabeation holding up faux groins which divide the vast hemispherical body into eight segments.

died in July 1576 at the age of 47. He did manage however to choose the architect and see his project laid out on paper. This was to be the house for his heirs.

In fact Vettor, who during the building phase in Bagnolo was little more than a young man, had decided not to commission Palladio, who was almost 70 and busy at the time with the Rotonda, but a brilliant 28-year-old architect from Vicenza, Vincenzo Scamozzi, who was practically two generations younger than Palladio and extremely different from the grand old master.

Palladio, the son of a miller, Pietro della Gondola, a stonemason and a self-taught man, had had to work very hard before making a name for himself in the profession; Vincenzo, on the other hand, had studied in the recently founded diocesan seminary in Vicenza, had frequented the milieu of the Accademia Olimpica where he was given a thorough grounding in Humanism, and was in close contact with the world of the University of Padua (which boasted members such as Galileo) as well as the Counter-Reformation movement in Vicenza.

It was his father Giandomenico, a land surveyor, who started his son

off on architecture, and it was with his father that as early as 1568, when he was only 20, Vincenzo was working on the villa of Girolamo Ferramosca in Barbano, along the road between Vicenza and Padua. In 1574 he designed the grand Villa Villaverla for Count Leonardo Verlato. The villa, in the upper Vicenza district, was a classically rigorous building. What's more, Vincezo perfected his education during his frequent trips in Italy and Europe – so much so, in fact, that he was appreciated as a sublime architect, hydraulic engineer

between the internal and external aspects and the functional practicality of the living quarters.

The site, which already contained the remains of a former fort, plays a fundamental role in terms of the panoramic views it affords, which span from the Alps to the Po Valley, and make the Rocca a sort of Acropolis-like temple enclosed within its rigid architectural scheme. The sense of isolation is further underscored by the long perspectival thrust of the straight road that leads to the Rocca, which leads to a large staircase that in turn

and treatisist well beyond the Veneto. He was responsible for the Procuratie Nuove in Venice, the perspectival views of the Teatro Olimpico in Vicenza (originally for Sophocles' *Oedipus Rex*) and the court theatre of Sabbioneta, commissioned by Vespasiano Gonzaga.

But he was to give the true mark of his genius with the Rocca Pisana. He undertook comparison with the Rotonda in the overall layout with cupola, but found a completely original solution in the spatial relationship

leads to a hexastyle pronaos concluded by a triangular fronton running along the main façade.

The other façades are given their rhythm only by the rigorously organised window openings with very simple flat surrounds and the central Serlian openings on the *piano nobile* which are subdivided by severely Ionic columns (like those of the pronaos), while the balustrades along the parapet are reminiscent of an "archaic" quadrangular typology which is similar to the one used by Falconetto and

Cornaro in the preceding Villa dei Vescovi in Luvigliano. The rigorous volumetric scale of the Rocca, whose corners are marked and reinforced with bushhammered quoins, is concluded with an octagonal drum on which rests the segmented cupola, opening up at its peak with a large oculus that floods the central room with light, and where the perspectives extend towards the entrance loggia and the side Serlian openings. The interior is remarkable for the purity of its surfaces, cut by the evident frames surrounding the openings, the Roman tassels of the fireplaces, the moulding of the ceilings and the flow of the stone slabs on the floor.

The Rocca's central plan was then taken up again by Scamozzi, albeit to less surprising effect, in the Molin Villa in Mandria (near Padua), in the no longer extant Villa Bardellini in Monfumo and the project for a villa that was to be built between Stra and Dolo, published along with other designs in the 1615 treatise *L'idea dell'architettura universale*.

Slightly apart from the villa there are a stable and guesthouse, also designed by Scamozzi, according to a late-16th-century custom whereby the servants' quarters and other non-residential buildings were moved away from the main building, thus separating the functional and the formal, which were characteristics of the villa culture.

The Rocca Pisana, after having been abandoned for more than a century (and during which period the acroterial statues along the tympanum disappeared), was restored in the post-War period by the Counts de' Lazara Pisani, direct descendants of the original owners. It was then bequeathed to the current owners, the Ferri counts. The simple and rigorous layout of the park, where there is a beautiful well-head, can also be traced back to the Lazaras, and dates from the 1950s.

Villa Contarini

Piazzola sul Brenta

Above: aerial view of the villa, highlighting the late-19th century design of the parterre, back garden.

Opposite page: detail of the ground-floor western loggia, with Serliana, rusticated doors and ornate pictorial decoration.

The locality known as Placiola, Plazola or Plateola, seems to be cited in documents from as early as the 13th century as belonging to the city of Vicenza. Here there was a fortified enclosure controlled by the Dente family, then handed over to the Belludi and then the Carraresi families.

It was a Carrara, Maria, daughter of Jacopo and Lucia Contarini, who in 1413 brought Piazzola as part of her dowry to the patrician Nicolò Contarini, a descendant of one of the twelve *case vecchie*, also known as *case apostoliche*, the oldest and most

powerful of the patrician clans in Venice (they were to provide, over the years, eight Doges, forty-four St Mark procurators and a cardinal).

Nicolò belonged to the Contarinis of San Cassiano, from the parish their home was in, who later became the San Trovaso Contarinis when they changed residence. They are, however, better known as the Scrigni Contarinis, an obvious allusion to the family's financial activity.

The official demands on such an illustrious and wealthy family led to the building of Villa Piazzola. Work began in 1546 when Francesco and Paolo Contarini oversaw the foundations of the current villa by building a *palazzo* that, except for minor additions and changes, then became the central block for the current complex. There are traces of the old Carrara fort in the podium and parts of the ramparts on which the villa was erected.

According to a tradition that dates back to 1681, when two works were published on the villa, the project was put together by Andrea Palladio. This hypothesis, more suggestive than real, was dictated by the family's self-commemorative intentions, which

Opposite page: detail of ornate late-17th-century decorations characterising the eastern wing, Villa Contarini.

Below: view of the romantic park, which extends from the back of the Piazzola villa and covers the old rice paddies belonging to the Contarini family.

culminated in the second half of the 17th century when Marco Contarini, procurator since 1662, an advocate of the Jesuits and husband to Elisabetta Contarini (perfectly in keeping with the tradition of marriages between blood relatives), began massive restructuring and extension work to turn Villa Piazzola into the grandest in the whole region.

Around 1674, the long right wing was radically transformed. Respectful of overblown baroque taste, the villa was given an elaborate balustrade and sculptural decorations. More than a century later, in 1788, the left wing was reworked and a passageway was added that led to the semicircular porticos in the square (the porticos, unfortunately, were never completed). A seigneurial chapel was built in 1770 by Tommaso Temanza from Venice.

The building programme begun by Marco Contarini is consistent with the exquisitely celebratory intents of the baroque, and even though we are not sure who was responsible for the final effect, there is some consistency to the idea that it was Alessandro Tremignon, a native of

*Previous page: the villa's simple
yet majestic back façade.*

*Left: fossa Contarina delimited
by the long balustrade punctuated by statues.
In the background, the old guesthouse
and the connecting passage to the porticoed
loggias in the piazza.*

the area who had worked on the San Moisè façade in Venice, where the decorative emphasis is very similar to the one found in Piazzola.

The interior was decorated in 1684 by Michele Primon from Padua. In part they take their inspiration from Pirro Ligorio's Roman subjects, and in part from Giulio Romano's Mantuan subjects.

Everything seems to be ready for the procurator Contarini to display the greatest pomp in receiving Ernest

The stables built by the Camerini dukes, 1920s.

August, the Duke of Brunswick, in 1685. *L'orologio del piacere*, by Francesco Maria Piccioli, published for the occasion, describes the theatrical and musical works performed "on earth and on water", including a naval battle between a Turkish and two Venetian vessels.

This taste for spectacle can also be seen in the villa's central hall on the ground floor, the so-called *sala delle audizioni*.

The room is surrounded by a gallery which communicates, via an

Below: detail of the so-called Sala delle Cariatidi, where monochrome male caryatids hold up faux stages with depictions of episodes from the history of the Tuccia vestal virgin, attributed to the Paduan artist Michele Primon and dated 1684.

Opposite page: detail of the Stanza del Baccanale, decorated with frescoes attributed to Michel Primon and painted circa 1684, obviously inspired by similar paintings by Giulio Romano in Palazzo Te, Mantua.

octagonal opening, with the room above, known as the *sala della chitarra rovesciata* because of its characteristic shape. This room has four balconies for instrumentalists.

As well as two theatres, an orphanage (called the *loco delle vergini*) for poor girls from honest families, a printery where opera librettos were published, Marco Contarini also installed a silk factory and metal-works, demonstrating incredible entrepreneurial skills. The orphanage also contained a music conservatory and workshops for lacemaking, tapestry and arrases.

The Contarinis ended their "reign" in 1836, and Piazzola was inherited by Andrea and Pierfrancesco Giovanelli and Giovanni Correr.

In 1852, after a period of decline and expropriation, the property was bought by Silvestro Camerini, from Castel Bolognese in Ravenna. Camerini was of extremely modest extraction, but had such extraordinary business skills that he was in fact the leading figure in the Italian economy of the period – so much so, in fact, that Pope Pius IX gave him the title of Duke.

In 1866 Piazzola was inherited by

Opposite page: central ground-floor hall with stuccoed 18th-century decorations.

Left: perspectival view of the balustrade in the central ground-floor hall, with details of the octagonal opening between the hall and the upstairs room, known as the Sala delle Chitarre.

his nephew Luigi Camerini, who had participated in the Risorgimento riots of 1848. He had the *parterres* in front of the villa restructured and had a small commemorative chapel built in honour of his uncle. The property was then bequeathed to his son Paolo, famous for his philanthropy as well as his astute economic nous. Following in his father's and great-uncle's footsteps, he had the villa restored and added new decorations by Pajetta, Torti and Zonaro as well as a new art collection with its own gallery and a library.

It was thanks to Paolo Camerini, a progressive Liberal, that the Italian economy boomed in this period. He was elected to the Italian parliament in 1892, and at the same time the building was transformed into a small factory, even though crop cultivation continued. The Piazzola holding in this period had grown to an incredible 10,000 hectares, divided into equally-sized plots with modern farm houses, roads and irrigation canals. The population grew from 1,900 in 1890 to 4,000 in 1914 (the whole catchment area in fact had a population that went from 5,500 to 10,000 in the same period).

It was Contarini who introduced the irrigation canals onto the property, and they were used to provide water for the fishing pond behind the villa and the small lake in the large landscape park the Camerinis had built over the rice fields originally flanking the villa.

Since 1970, the Piazzola villa has belonged to the Fondazione Culturale G E Ghirardi, which has undertaken radical restoration and conservation work on the building.

Left: the Scala dei Giganti in the western wing, with overblown Neo-baroque decorations attributed to Vincenzo Torti, built between 1878-1880.

Below: the ball room with stucco decorations and frescoed allegories, with the wall and ceiling frescoes attributed to Girolamo Pellegrini.
The fireplace has a reproduction of Michelangelo's tomb for Lorenzo de Medici in the new sacristy of the church of San Lorenzo, Florence.

Villa Barbarigo
Valsanziobio

Below: aerial view of part of Valsanzibio's garden, highlighting the two main axes subdividing the park.

Opposite page: the composite façade giving on to the garden, Villa Barbarigo.

Giovan Francesco Barbarigo, from one of the most important *case nuove* which provided two Doges, ten St Mark's procurators and four cardinals, began at the end of the 16th century to inherit and buy land in the Colli Euganei district, in Valsanzibio, that is in the little valley of San Zibio or Eusebio, the patron saint of the little church in the village just below Praglia Abbey.

The lands at Valsanzibio originally belonged to Giacomo Scrovegni, the rich money-lending family from Padua that had commissioned the Madonna dell'Arena, Eremitani, chapel from Giotto. His property had been confiscated when he was accused of treason, and were sold off in 1440 to the Venetian Lodovico Contarini, who was succeeded by the patricians Michiel, Ferro, Bolani and Bragadin and then the Barbarigos from Santa Maria Zobenigo who, thanks to a helping hand from the Paduan clergy, eventually won succession rights. The area was particularly amenable with a large water supply. An intricate network of rivers and streams linked the site to Padua and Venice, and

there was a more than decorous seigneurial settlement there. The Sienese astronomer Alessandro Piccolomini sang the praises of the buildings, land and fishing ponds in 1529. During the 1630 Plague, this is where the Barbarigo family came for their quarantine period, even though there is more detailed information on Giovan Francesco Barbarigo and his son Antonio only from 1661 on. The decision to renovate the Valsanzibio property was probably taken by Antonio, Venetian senator and St Mark's procurator, brother to Cardinal Gregorio who became bishop of Padua in 1664. Work began in the early 1660s, according to a plan by an unknown architect, and lasted until at least the end of the century.

The plan, now on display in a frame from the period, originally included new buildings and a typically classical late-Renaissance garden over a rectangular plot of land divided into four equal strips, each of which in turn divided into four square modules of 40x40 metres, punctuated by parallel and octagonal avenues. This thus formed 24 "green rooms", or episodes, according to a structure that brought together

pure entertainment elements (such as *jeux d'eau*) and philosophical-symbolic elements, which were evident in the inscriptions on the pedestals of statues representing Parnassian divinities and allegories from the 16th-century treatise repertory.

The excessively ambitious nature of the project, and perhaps even direct intervention from Cardinal Barbarigo (opposed to any display of lavishness during the Counter-Reformation), meant that the western and southern garden modules were never completed, and explains why the villa, itself never completed, is so simple.

In 1804, on the death of Contarina Barbarigo, Valsanzibio was inherited by his cousin Marcantonio Michiel, who then included it in his daughter Cecilia's dowry, which then went to Count Lodovico Martinengo da Barco. Thanks to Martinengo, the garden is partially transformed according to current Romantic tastes, and exotic species and thick wooded areas were added to the woods that had grown wild over the original walls. Partial restoration work began in the 1920s on behalf of the Donà dalle Rose family and continued by the noble Pizzoni Ardemani family, who have owned the complex since 1929. The centre of the approximately 14-hectare garden is represented by the *Fontana della Pila*, surrounded by statues of Argus and

Mercury, the garden's custodians, and by allegories of Salubriousness and Fecundity. This is where the north-south axis running from the villa meets with the east-west axis running from the *Bagno di Diana*, the original entrance to the garden. This is a pavilion which faces onto a small pond which has relatively recently replaced the old through road.

To the sides of the central gate there are two niches with the statues of Atheone and Endymion, Diana's lovers. Diana herself dominates the scene from the centre of the fastigium which is linked with the broken overhanging tympanum. A recurring decorative motif is the sunflower, a neo-Platonic symbol of consciousness and knowledge. From the podium constituted by the internal perspectival view of the *Bagno di Diana*, where there are towering statues of Jove, Mercury and Hercules, there is a series of small ponds. The first is called the *Peschiera dei Fiumi*, with allegorical statues of the

Left: the sequence of pools along the "water route" with, respectively, the Peschiera dei Fiumi, the Fontana del Cigno, the Peschiera dei Venti, the Fontana della Pila and, in the background, the 19th-century Bacino dei Pesci Rossi.

Right: the elliptical Isola dei Conigli, with central bird-cage.

Below: the façade giving on to the countryside of the so-called Bagno di Diana, one of Valsanzibio's most successful architectural caprices, with large pool from the 1950s.

Brenta and Bacchiglione rivers. It is followed by the *Fontana del Cigno*, whose jets of water represented the iris, and the *Peschiera dei Venti*, with grottoes surmounted by statues of Aeolus and various nymphs. Beyond the slightly raised *Fontana della Pila* there is the last of the pools, known as the *Peschiera dei Pesci Rossi*, created in the 19th century by the Martinengos and replacing the *parterre* representing the Barbarigo coat-of-arms. In that period, the garden was famous for its variety of rare species of cultivated flowers (there were a whole 226 different species), as well as fruit trees (233 in all), which were all exhaustively listed in a manuscript. In the southern part of the garden there are a labyrinth and small 19th-century woods.

In the modules near the villa there are two very odd "green rooms" with a central oval plan: in the eastern one there is a statue of Time, represented as a winged bearded giant holding aloft a heavy polyhedron. The following distich is inscribed on the pedestal: *with time fly the hours, and flee the years*. In the western "room", however, there is an elliptical *Isola dei Conigli* (Island of Rabbits) surrounded by a moat, with a central aviary called the *Castello delle Tortore* (Castle of Turtle Doves).

Typical for a baroque garden is the *Fontana degli scherzi d'acqua* (the *jeux d'eau*), situated in the north-south avenue. The fountain is surrounded by four statues alternating references to good and evil – the negative figures of Polyphemus and Typheus are juxtaposed with the benevolent allegories of Flora and Ope.

In the centre of the courtyard in front of the villa, and raised just enough to be able to dominate the area below, there is the *Fontana del Delfino o del Fungo*, a symbol of divine ecstasy, surrounded by a series of allegorical statues representing Delight, Happiness, Indolence, Agriculture, Genius, Harmony, Blessed Solitude, Abundance and then Adonis, who perhaps represents ambition.

The garden's fame and popularity even while it was being constructed was due to a book called *Le fabbriche e giardini di casa Barbarigo*, published by Domenico Rossi in 1702.

The fifteen incisions included in the text show important episodes from the garden constructed by the procurator Barbarigo. The patrician's own reasons for putting together such an extraordinary garden can be found in the engraved lines in each of the seven gardens (as many as the planets known by the Ancients) which lead to the secret garden in front of the villa:

You who arrive full of curiosity, and who walk around in search of rare entertainment,
observe, and say, that, even though one appear, it is all the work of Nature and not of Art.
Here the glorious Sun its rays imparts, here Venus most beautiful rises from the Sea:
here her mutations the moon provides all the clearer, here there is no Mars his fury to disturb us.
Here Saturn desists from gnawing his offspring, her Jove is jovial, and his Face serene; here Mercury his deceits leaves behind. Here there is no crying, and laughter reigns; here the clap of Courtly thunder cannot be heard; here is hell, and here is Paradise.

Villa Allegri Arvedi

Cuzzano

Aerial view of the Cuzzano complex, with sequence of ramparted garden, the villa, the back courtyard, and the San Carlo chapel.

Opposite page: the Baroque façade of the villa designed in 1656 by Giovan Battista Bianchi for the Allegri degli Honorij counts.

In the north-eastern district behind Verona there is the Valpantena, formed by two rivers, the Vajo dell'Anguilla and the Falconi, squeezed into a long high-banked canal which widens towards the city to form a broad valley dotted with villas that have bloomed and become the governing centres for vast agricultural concerns.

In the locality of Cuzzano, just before the main village of Grezzena along the gentle slope that rises towards the hill, there was a fortified house, perhaps a tower, owned by the Scala family. It was then inherited by the Vermes, a powerful arms family whose properties were expropriated many times by Venice because of their antagonism to the Republic; the property was then passed on to the Allegre degli Honorii family. This latter family, present in Verona since the 13th century with houses in Contrada San Vitale, was admitted to the city's Noble Council in 1406, when Verona fell under the thrall of Venice. One of the most distinguished members of the family was Annibale, who climbed the ranks in St Mark's army until he became *condottiero di gente d'armi* and, in 1604 at the age of 26, married Bartolomea Clusoni, a 72-year-old widow and owner of an "immense legacy of more than 40,000 ducats". The family's upward social mobility continued with George III, who was also a *condottiero* for the Republic of Venice, who was given the title of Count by the Serenissima in 1624 along with feudal prerogatives over Fagnan and Nogarole, which he could pass on to his legitimate heirs. His son Giovan Battista then began to rework and extend the old Cuzzano houses

Left: seigneurial chapel, with staircases and loggias.

*Above: details of formal garden with volutes,
large box trees shaped like cones and cupolas.*

in 1656. He chose the architect and sculptor Giovan Battista Bianchi, born in Verona in 1631 to a family of stone cutters and altar builders. In all likelihood he did his apprenticeship in his father's workshop, but what is certain is that the youngster soon showed his talent for architecture – at the age of only 25 he was chosen by as important a commission as the one working on Villa Cuzzano.

As has already been pointed out, there was a fortified building on the site. Although this old building had been reworked many times, the architect wanted to maintain reference to the building's quadrilateral shape by including four side towers. Even the wall surrounding the garden and the western wing of the villa, resting on an ancient barbican podium, invite the same conclusion, as does the wall structure of the cellar, the dungeons and the large ashlar stone arches in the southern portion of the left wing. As for the stylistic choices, Bianchi moved away from the 16th century

Neoclassicism which was dominant in the Verona of the period and embraced the novelty of the baroque, which he interpreted masterfully (see the altars he designed for several churches in Verona and Mantua, such as Santa Teresa, as well as Bologna, such as San Michele in Bosco agli Scalzi). At Cuzzano he constructed a building articulated according to different volumes, with the main façade characterised by a five-opening portico on lateral ashlar columns and pilasters, holding up a wide terrace surrounded by a balustrade. The middle section of the villa is punctuated by Doric semi-columns which hold up a high trabeation with metopes and triglyphs, on which there are six telamones which give rhythm to the attic. The attic is closed off by a stone balustrade decorated with statues, which were probably sculpted by Bianchi himself. Bianchi was also responsible for the complex scroll held aloft by putti, the central part of which contained the heraldic coat-of-arms of the Allegris,

Opposite page: magnificent ground-floor hall with faux-architecture decorations showing battle scenes and allegories of the signs of the zodiac, frescoed by Ludovico Dorigny, 1717-1720.

Above: detail showing Perseus and the Medusa.

which has since worn away. Two wings with terraces, protected once more by balustrades with statues, link the villa to the two side towers surmounted by spires, an explicit reference to the military nobility boasted by the "gens Honoria", as the Allegris liked to call themselves.

To the back of the building there is a courtyard surrounded by servants' quarters and other buildings which are also protected by towers. The courtyard is also closed off by the seigneurial chapel dedicated to San Carlo Borromeo, which is preceded by a double staircase. The lateral loggias to the chapel, closed off by a large mixtilinear fastigium in turn crowned by volutes and statues, and the campanile with onion dome designed by Giovan Battista Bianchi, were built after Bianchi's death in 1687. The right wing of the villa towards the garden is concluded by a pavilion which houses a large frescoed aviary with vegetable motif and a grottoed room with shells, stalactites, fountain and the sculptural groups of *Hercules and the Hydra* and *Hercules and Cerberus*.

The formal garden is also worthy of note. It opens up in front of the villa and extends over a ramparted terrace with watchtowers in each corner. Enormous box bushes, trimmed to the shape of a cupola and cone, surround the garden where very low box hedges and coloured gravel form an elaborately patterned *parterre* with French volutes, according to a scheme that probably dates back to the 18th century.

Much more recent is the avenue of cypresses and trimmed box bushes that leads from the porter's lodge.

The interior of the villa has many rooms with ceilings with painted beams and frescoed decorations by the Veronese painters Sante Prunati and Giuseppe Falezza. The oldest frescoes (which have often been touched up) in a ground floor room are by Paolo Farinati.

A veritable theatre is the large hall on the *piano nobile*, which is entirely decorated with faux architectural motifs accompanied, in the lower order, by allegories of the signs of the zodiac and warring giants. In the upper section of the walls there are two large frescoed scenes respectively representing *Perseus and the Medusa* and *The Battle between Centaurs and Lapites*. The author of the frescoes, which date back to 1717-1720, is the French artist Lodovico Dorigny, son of the painter Michel and maternal grandson of the more famous Simon Vouet. Born in Paris in 1654, after completing his apprenticeship with the painter Charles Le Brun, Dorigny spent a lot of time in Rome and Venice, where he worked for the Zenobios and Manins, two families which had only recently been included in the list of patrician families. These families' celebratory demands were met by the young French artist, who provided magniloquent compositions.

The incredible decorative structure in the Cuzzano hall has led some to think that the faux architectural motifs are the work of Francesco Galli da Bibbiena, who in that period was supervising work on the Philharmonic Theatre in Verona.

The chapel must also be noted for the complex frescoed decorations, undertaken once again by Dorigny.

In 1824, the Cuzzano property was handed over by the last of the Allegris, Lucrezia, to the Trent silk merchant Giovanni Antonio Arvedi. In 1828, Arvedi intended to transform the villa into a silk mill. He thankfully abandoned the idea and decided to keep the house for official receptions and as an agricultural base. This has been respected by the current descendants and owners.

Villa Fracanzan Piovene

Orgiano

Opposite page: the façade giving on to the hill, seen from the garden exedra.

Above: aerial view of Villa Fracanzan, Orgiano, with massive central body (1710), the long barchessa by Muttoni and the rustic courtyard of the 15th-century fortified nucleus.

Orgiano, an ancient town specialising in hemp production, situated partly on the Vicentine plain and partly on the slopes of the southern hills of the Colli Berici, derives its name from the original Latin Aurelianum, from the Aureli family, who owned the lands assigned to them in the district by the emperor Augustus in the 1st century CE as part of a series of payoffs to faithful centurions and veterans.

The name Aurelianum was then modified to Orglanum because of the orgiastic rites organised there in honour of Bacchus, to whom a temple had been dedicated in the area. Then the name of Orgiano was given by the emperor Ottone III to the bishop of Vicenza, who was also given the titles of duke, marquis and count. The bishop himself bequeathed the land he had been given as fifes to important local families. Thus in 1412, the Vicentine Fracanzan family, who boasted direct descent from Gondimaro, the first king of Burgundy, was given the lands of Orgiano, which they held for more than 300 years. The town was also seat of the Vicariate, that is a magistrate with administrative and jurisdictional functions, who was elected annually from among the members of Vicenza's Noble Council. The Fracanzans were not only members of this council, but over the years they would provide many Vicariates for the town of Orgiano. One of these, in the early 18th century, was Count Francesco Fracanzan, whose policy it was to consolidate the family's property, which ultimately led to his son's decision to build the current villa.

The site is to the margins of the residential area of the town, and slightly

Left: detail of the façade giving on to the countryside, with tetrastyle loggia.

Above left: perspectival view of the garden, as seen from the villa.

Above right: the villa seen from the long hornbeam-lined drive.

raised along the main road that leads to Vicenza along the Berico hills. This is where the Fracanzans had always had their homes, and can still be identified in the rustic courtyard to the east of the 1710 complex. The age of the settlement is also testified to by the tower, which contains gothic elements beneath the different layers of 16th- and 18th-century restorations, which can be seen in the Romantic crenellations.

Even though there is no documentary evidence, Giovan Battista Fracanzan, Francesco's son, turned to the architect Francesco Muttoni, born in Cima di Porlezza (Comasco) in 1668, the son of the architect Defendente. After he moved to Vicenza, the young Francesco was profoundly influenced by the work of Palladio, who had died about a century before. This can be evinced from the persistent classical severity of his work. Amongst his works there are the Bertoliana library in Vicenza, the plan for a restructuring of the entrance porticos at the sanctuary on Monte Berico and Villa Favorita at Monticello di Fara and Villa Valmarana Morosini at Altavilla Vicentina. But there are also many notes that recall Borromini, whose

works Francesco studied during his trip to Rome in 1708.

In Orgiano, Muttoni chose to build the new residence for the Fracanzans in the centre of the land, at the feet of the amphitheatre, thus taking advantage of the double opening onto the countryside and onto the public street.

The main, squared body was built as an isolated structure in order to exalt the monumental nature of the project. The main façade, preceded by a dramatic staircase that links the road level to the hall of the *piano nobile*, is squared off by two small octagonal corner towers; there is also a rococo entrance gate and the elevation of the dormer window which is rounded off by a triangular fronton in classical style. The seigneurial chapel, situated on the other side of the road, was built in 1688.

The old-fashioned open-air theatre, known as the *Casa dell'Orologio*, was built only in the 19th century, mainly for reasons of symmetry with the chapel. Its *fons scenae* is the façade of the villa itself.

More indebted to the baroque tastes of the period is the southern façade, which looks out over the garden, and particularly its central portion with, along the ground floor, its three openings in the rusticated ashlar plaster work, and a high tetrastyle loggia which covers the two upper floors. Above the loggia there is a high attic floor used as a granary, with a central arched opening and an elaborate baroque fronton with volutes. The villa is linked with the old courtyard, and hence rotated if compared to the residential part of the building, via an imposing ashlar-arched barchessa, punctuated by two trabeated structures that are repeated at either end.

The interior of the villa has substantially large rooms, above all in the central section of the ground floor, which is subdivided into three naves by two rows of pillars, and in the hall on the *piano nobile*, marked by lateral monumental doors surmounted by stucco fastigia. The side rooms on the ground floor have impressive vaulted ceilings linked with the walls by visible shelving. One of the most interesting rooms is the kitchen, with its incredible décor and red marble sink with lion's-head taps. Facing the villa's façade there is a quadrangular garden with large yew trees and two fountains. This is where the kilometre-long perspectival avenue begins, flanked by four files of hornbeams and ornamental stone vases.

Previous page: the ground-floor atrium held aloft by pilasters and divided into three naves.

Above left: detail of the so-called Salotto del Plebiscito.
Below: the ball room on the piano nobile.

The two large fish ponds, which cut across the rows of hornbeams, are not just a decorative element; they also provide the water for the villa's farming land.

Beside the residential unit, towards the town, the old *jardin potager* has recently been restored. It is surrounded by pergolas with orchard and fruit trees. The Orgiano complex was passed on by the Fracanzans to the dal Ferro, Orgiano and Marsilio families, after which it was inherited by Countess Francesca Piovene Porto Godi, who, along with her husband Nicolò Giusti del Giardino, has supervised the villa's restoration.

Left: the ground-floor kitchen with its characteristic ceiling, covered in centuries-old soot.

Above: the ground-floor dining room, with Roman-style tassel.

Villa Bertolo Valmarana

Vicenza

Right: aerial view of the Nani complex, with the squared structure of the stables in the foreground, followed by the small palazzo with rear garden containing a niche dedicated to Neptune.

Opposite page: the stables by Francesco Muttoni, 1730s.

Page 212: the Nani palazzina with view of the rear garden, the entrance gates and the long sequence of dwarves along the enclosing wall.

Page 213: the pagoda in the villa's Romantic park.

Villa dei Nani, or dwarves, is just outside the eastern gates to the city, on the Poggio di San Bastian, which takes its name from the 15th century church that was originally on the site but was destroyed during the period of Napoleonic religious suppression (there are still signs of its presence in the garden of the villa belonging to the Franco counts). The Nani complex is therefore situated at the very head of the Riviera Berica, quite close to the Rotonda, with which it is linked by means of a footpath.

The first building, completed in 1670, was built thanks to Giovanni Maria Bértolo, the famous Serenissima jurist whose main residence was in Venice. A committed book-lover, he virtually founded the Bertoliana library in Vicenza by donating his entire collection. The small seigneurial *palazzo* in Bértolo's time was a simple building, and harked back to the Venetian style of Giuseppe Sardi, which basically provided a single floor built over a high podium with a mezzanine floor above.

On his death in 1707, the complex also included a barchessa, guesthouse, stable, terrace with stone statues,

courtyard, well, garden and citrus garden. It was inherited by the Ognissanti convent in Padua, where Bértolo's only daughter, Giulia, was a nun. After 1720, the much-declined property was handed over to the Valmarana brothers. The Valmarana family, who still own the complex, were given the title of count by Corrado II and the title of Paduan counts by Charles V in 1540; the family was included in the list of Venetian patricians in 1658. It was Giustino Valmarana who took the complex in hand and in 1736 he called on Francesco Muttoni, a Comasco architect who had been working in the

Vicenza region for years, to undertake restoration and restructuring. Muttoni is responsible for embellishing the small *palazzo*, whose two façades were provided with small triangular tympana and acroterial statues and the small baroque cupola on the small lateral tower containing the interior staircases.

Muttoni's work is more evident in the long guesthouse with blind ashlared arches (although it is thought that they were originally open), to which the entrance atrium with Tuscan columns is linked. His masterpiece, however, is the stables, a square-planned building

Left: the central hall in the palazzina with frescoes by Giambattista Tiepolo based on Iphigenia's sacrifice.

Below: the Stanza dell'Orlando Furioso with, to the left, Angelica and Medoro taking their leave from the peasants and, to the right, Angelica helping the wounded Medoro, by Giambattista Tiepolo, 1757.

Page 216: detail of the Stanza dell'Olimpo in the guesthouse showing the conversation between Venus, Eros and Mars, by Giambattista Tiepolo.

Page 217: Detail of Iphigenia's sacrifice in the passage hall to the villa entrance showing the soothsayer interrupting the sacrifice in front of a shocked crowd, while Agamemnon covers his face with his cloak.

preceded by an ashlared portico with Serlian arches, with a large bearded head on the keystone, surmounted by a triangular fronton with decorative vases. The ground floor room of the stables is particularly well-made, with its three naves, divided by supports, which is echoed in the cross-vaults of the ceiling. The lack of buildings for the agricultural business of the villa, which are relegated to isolated positions or are left freestanding in far flung areas, further underscores the residential nature of Villa dei Nani. The garden was definitively reorganised between 1772 and 1785 by Countess Elena Garzadori, wife of Count Gaetano Valmarana. The geography of the site, which is a sort of long flatland interrupted by small *palazzi*, conditioned the architecture of the garden, which is divided into a front section, which acts as a link between

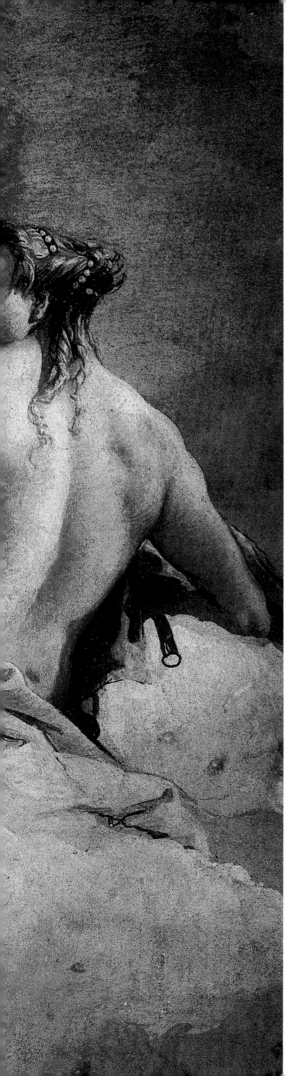

the entrance pavilion, the guesthouse and the villa, and a back section. The axial structure, which goes from the monumental entrance to the small *piazza* (which matches the perspectival position of the opposite entrance to the nearby Villa Franco), and then continues through the small *palazzi*, along the double row of hornbeams in the back garden. A fountain with a monumental statue of Neptune is to be found in the dramatic layout with rusticated ashlar and tympanum which closes off the long perspectival view. Towards the *Valletta del Silenzio*, flanking the southern side of the villa, there is a long land terrace, with the remains of a citrus garden, just below the level of the garden. Another land terrace occupying a third level is home to the vegetable garden. Just beneath the small tower with cupola there is a *ciacolesso*, that is a sort of open-air salon formed by trimmed box bushes in the shape of seats. There is a well in the middle of the garden, while the side giving on to the valley is closed off by a scenic view frescoed onto a wall with faux architectural motifs and a wonderful marble fountain. In the thick woods that go from the opposite end of the property to beyond the stables there is a late-18th

century pagoda pavilion which was in keeping with the *chinoiserie* tastes of the period.

The wall which closes off the garden from the public road is interrupted by two ashlar gates finished off with fastigia with decorative vases. Along this wall, punctuated by rusticated pilasters, there are seventeen statues of dwarves, from which the villa's name derives.

The sculptor in question is Francesco Uliaco, who had learnt his trade in the famous Vicenza workshop of the Marinalis. Dwarves, which were seen to be part of the grotesque canon, can be found in the rather popular engravings of the French artist Jacques Callot, in the Commedia dell'Arte and in the works of Giambattista Tiepolo and above all in the works of his son Giandomenico, both of whom were called on to decorate the interior of the villa and guesthouse.

Count Giustino, making a public display of where his affections lay, chose San Bastian as his main residence, and this perhaps explains why he lavished so much money on it. Love and the call to duty are the themes of the frescoes chosen for the villa, and are derived from episodes taken from the *Iliad*, *Orlando Furioso*, the *Aeneid* and *Gerusalemme Liberata*, thus alternating classical and modern epics. Giambattista Tiepolo, who was working on his third commission in the Vicenza area after the frescoes for Villa Loschi in Biròn (1734) and the frescoes for the Cordellina in Montecchio Maggiore (1743-1744), was assisted by his son Giandomenico and the *trompe-l'oeil* painter Girolamo Mengozzi Colonna.

Colonna, an expert scenographer from Ferrara, managed to transform the modest spaces within the house with a series of faux columns on the central room, also known as the Iphigenia staircase, and in the *Sala di Achille*, and with imaginative baroque surrounds in the other rooms. In amongst the decorations by Colonna, which have the function of involving the viewer, there are paintings by Giambattista Tiepolo, who alternates epic mastery and more intimate moments and an immensely luminous chromatic scale. The frescoes in the guesthouse, which is a series of seven aligned rooms facing onto the entrance hall, are all by Giandomenico except for those in the *Sala dell'Olimpo*, in the centre of the suite, which are by his father.

Mengozzi Colonna is once again responsible for the frames, which include rococo, exotic and neogothic elements. The *passeggiata estiva* (summer's walk) and the *passeggiata invernale* (winter's walk) in the *Stanza Gotica* and the re-evocations of labouring farmers in the *Stanza Campestre* are very suggestive. The themes were chosen by Giandomenico Tiepolo who preferred the daily life as seen in Gozzi's fables and Goldoni's comedies to classical literature.

Antonio Fogazzaro, Margherita di Valmarana's husband, described Villa dei Nani in his *Piccolo mondo moderno*, even though he called it Villa Diedo.

Villa Pompei Sagramoso

Illasi

Girolamo Pompei, known as Malanchino, offered his services to the Republic and joined other recruits in the Lessinia valley in the Cambrai War. A little luck and much audacity led to his capturing, near Isola della Scala in the lower Verona district, the marquis of Mantua, Francesco Gonzaga, who was allied with the imperial forces during the war.

This happened on August 8th, 1509; on October 12th of the same year, the Venetian Senate, considering their loyalty and merits acquired by the family, gave Girolamo Pompei and his brothers the fife of Illasi with *usque poenam sanguinis* rights and the title of Counts of Illasi. This investiture became effective only in 1516, when Venice regained full control over the mainland.

The Pompeis thus settled in the castle at Illasi, which was strategically positioned on a hill that afforded a complete view of the Adige valley and plain.

The castle, in fact, was really a keep and a tower, surrounded by elliptical walls which had been restored by the Scaligeri family after they had been destroyed by Ezzelino da Romano in 1239. The castle, however, which was

Above: aerial view of the Illasi complex clearly showing the western wing, which was left untouched in the 18th-century restructuring, and the Italian garden with greenhouses.

Opposite page: detail of the ground-floor entrance to the villa.

Illasi, the main town in the eponymous valley which characterises eastern Lessinia in the pre-Alpine district of Verona, is historically linked to the Pompei family, who were already well-known during the Scaligeri period and part of the city's Noble Council in 1410, that is at the very beginning of the Serenissima.

The Pompeis were one of the very few noble subjected families who unhesitatingly chose to back Venice during the Cambrai crisis, thus siding with the lower classes.

Left: the Illasi villa with eastern wing.

Below: details of the villa's "Moorish" greenhouses.

so far from the town, was not suitable for governing over the feudal lands.

The Pompeis thus abandoned it during the 16th century, and moved to a home at the foot of the hill. This home was a simple building embellished by a loggia, to which was added in 1675 a body with another loggia (Doric) along the first floor and painted and faux-ashlared plaster on the ground floor.

In the meantime, the family broke up into smaller factions who were given the names of the streets they lived in, but there were only two branches who shared jurisdiction over Illasi – the *Isolo di Sotto* and the *San Paolo in Campomarzo* branches.

The latter branch was given the family home in Contrada Castello, while the other branch moved to another villa in Contrada Piazza. A third branch, known as the *San Pietro Incarnario* branch, moved to Contrada dei Fani. These seigneurial settlements eventually characterised the entire town, which is structured around

Left: view of the large reception hall on the piano nobile.

Below: the ruins of Illasi castle overlooking the 19th-century park, Villa Pompei.

the noble villas with high stone walls surrounding the gardens and fields.

In the 1730s both main branches were busy renovating their respective Illasi residences, happily aping the Venetian patricians. Thus while the Isolo di Sotto Pompeis (who died out with the Carlotti marquises) called on a related architect, Alessandro Pompei, to put together a project based on a clearly Palladian classical design, the San Paolo in Campomarzo Pompeis turned to someone who had nothing to do with the family.

The renovation and extension of the old complex in Contrada Castello, begun in the 17th century, was in all probability the end result of a collaborative effort between two architects working in Verona – Giovan Pietro Pozzo and Vincenzo Pellesina. The latter is the more famous of the two. Pellesina worked on the completion of the Sanmicheli Palazzo Canossa in Verona, and designed a country residence in Valeggio sul Mincio for the Maffei counts. The Illasi villa, work on which continued until 1737, has a central body, incorporating the preceding 16th-century residence, with ashlar portico with five openings, with a corresponding sequence of architraved windows with ear-shaped modelled surrounds along the upper floors. The building then extends along two wings, the western one of which is in fact the old 1675 building, which was probably left untouched because of lack of funds. The eastern wing, however, has a portico and loggia with exactly the same stylistic elements as the main body. There are also noteworthy annexes, punctuated by blind arches on rusticated pilasters which surround the villa. The main courtyard is closed off by a scenic wing, opened in the centre by a gate that leads into the formal garden, and closed off at its two

Left: detail of one of the piano nobile living rooms.

Right: the so-called Camera Azzurra o del Vescovo.

Opposite page: the first-floor hall with pavilion ceiling with sumptuous faux-architectural decorations, by anonymous fresco artists, 1740-1745.

extremes by two monumental ashlar entrances surmounted by a triangular tympanum. The eastern entrance leads to the farmhouses and the park, while the other is in fact the main entrance to the complex. Much simpler is the sever façade of the building, which looks out over the park. The façade was begun in the 1830s by the last of the Pompeis, Antonio, who was an enthusiastic archaeologist and botanist. The area, which occupies an entire slope of Monte Tenda and contains the remains of the ancient castle, covers almost 30 hectares. It was radically transformed for the villa. Count Antonio enhanced elements from the preceding garden, such as the belvedere and the cypress-lined avenue leading to the castle, but also added new elements, including a lake in the same shape as Lake Garda and a new road suitable for vehicles which winds its way up the hill.

The castle, according to the taste for ruins of the period, became the pivot around which the rest of the composition was constructed.

Antonio Pompei also had greenhouses built in the Moorish style near the old formal garden behind the villa.

The interior of the building is perfectly in keeping with the sumptuousness of the exterior. The pavilioned ceilings in the reception rooms on the first floor, amongst which the largest is the ballroom, were decorated in about the 1740s by painters from the Verona entourage of Antonio Balestra.

The subjects chosen, which go from the fall of Phaeton in the main hall to Borea raping Orizia in the so-called cardinal's room, seem to form an organic cycle where the theme on the ceiling is determined by the direction of the room itself, thus constituting a sort of mythological map of the heavens.

The grand architectural decorations framing the mythological scenes are exemplary. Other ceilings in the eastern wing were decorated by Giambattista Cignaroli in 1739-1741, and display mythological figures.

About thirty years later, the Pompeis called on Marco Marcola to decorate the ceilings in the other rooms, and then, in 1785, the Veronese Giovanni Cannella, who frescoed a drawing room on the ground floor with scenes of the city with ancient architectural motifs, and Andrea Porta, who decorated the dining room on the ground floor with landscapes that are part of the painter's traditional repertoire.

The Illasi complex was inherited by the Perez counts on the death of Antonio Pompei in 1885. It was then bequeathed to the Sagramoso Perez Pompei counts, who are currently living there.

Villa Pisani

Stra

Above: aerial view of Villa Pisani, Stra,
by Francesco Maria Preti, 1730s.

Opposite page: detail of the middle episode
in the façade giving on to the Naviglio di Brenta,
Villa Pisani.

The Pisani family was already present at Rialto in the 9th century, and had almost certainly come from Eraclea and not from Pisa as the family name might suggest. Over the years the family branched out into different factions, and of these, the most conspicuous branch was that of Santo Stefano.

In 1724 their entire property was valued at 37,835 ducats, an enormous amount considering that 1,000 ducats was considered more than enough to keep a good patrician family in the style it was accustomed to.

Their city *palazzo* in Campo Santo Stefano, now the Conservatorio Benedetto Marcello, was begun in the early 17th century, and is one of the most imposing in Venice.

As early as the 17th century, the Pisani Santo Stefano family had started to buy lands at Stra, along the Naviglio di Brenta, which for centuries had been the communication channel between Venice and Padua. Their lordly residence appears from engravings by Coronelli (1709) and Volkamer (1714) to have been formed by a building with a bell-shaped roof, perhaps of Gothic origin, to which had been added a columned pronaos crowned by a mixtilinear baroque fronton.

These are the years in which the Riviera di Brenta, considered the "suburbs" of Venice, became the privileged place for the city's nobility to retire on their holidays. In the 18th century, in fact, the economy of the area was almost exclusively based on Venetian nobility holidaying in their villas.

Very soon, however, the Stra villa was considered inadequate for the needs and ambitions of the six Pisani brothers, amongst whom the most important were Almorò and Alvise.

Almorò, the elder, dedicated himself almost exclusively to looking after the family's estate, while Alvise was much more ambitious: from 1699 to 1704 he was ambassador to Paris, where the Sun King was godfather to his son. After other missions to England and Germany, he was nominated procurator of St Mark in 1711; in 1735 he was finally elected Doge, which he would continue to hold until his death in 1741.

It is in a historical period in which ostentation constituted the very emblem of power that we must collocate the social demands of the Pisanis, who, in the 1720s, started

*Left: the spectacular stables
by Frigimelica, with, in the foreground,
statues of Zephyr and Flora,
by Giovanni Bonazza.*

*Above: view of the façade giving
on to the garden.*

enormous extension and restoration work both on the Santo Stefano *palazzo* and the Stra villa.

They chose Girolamo Frigimelica Roberti to work on both. Frigimelica was from Padua, and was a cultured man with many interests, including travelling, writing librettos and designing theatrical sets. He elaborated an all-encompassing plan for the entire water-bed area on the Brenta, which required the demolition of the old villa and the construction of a grandiose new *palazzo* (the wooden model is still on display at the Museo

Correr in Venice). The latter took its inspiration from the work of Palladio, Longhena and Filippo Juvarra. It also provided for a spectacular stable and the planting of a vast garden based on the French models of Le Nôtre, with a central *allée* linking the villa and stable, and two axes cutting diagonally through the main axis. Building began in 1720, and lasted for years. Frigimelica supervised the construction even after he moved to Modena, where Duke Rinaldo III of Este invited him to be his son's private tutor and to be the official court poet. The garden was laid out during the initial phase, and it covered an incredible eleven hectares of land (the Pisanis continued to buy and add to their three lordly properties of Villa Codognola, Ca' Graziani, Ca' Toffetti) and included a wealth of statues, attributed to the Paduan workshop of the Bonazzas, and caprices: a labyrinth with a circular tower at its centre, a *caffeehaus* built on the knoll of the icehouse, a mixtilinear exedra with six arches linked to the two long structures of the gardener's residence and the old greenhouses.

Frigimelica also supervised the monumental entrances to the garden alongside the villa, which were similar to triumphal arches surmounted by hefty curvilinear tympana, with two rustic openings on either side. The *Portale del Belvedere* is a masterpiece of imagination and balance. It is flanked by two giant Corynthian columns, with, at its summit, allegorical statues of Spring and Autumn, around which wind the spiral staircases that lead to the terrace held aloft by the portal itself. Even the stables with a central pronaos with Ionic columns, surmounted by an attic with decorative statues and vases, testify to Frigimelia's spectacular deftness. He died in Modena in 1732, without ever having begun work on the *palazzo*.

When he died, the Pisanis turned to a young thirty-year-old architect from Castelfranco Veneto, where he had rebuilt the Duomo – Francesco Maria Preti. Preti never touched what his predecessor had already completed, but he did elaborate new projects for the villa. The Pisanis chose the one that was more in keeping with the nascent Classicism, articulated according to two porticoed courtyards flanking a central columned atrium. Work progressed so quickly that in 1735, when Alvise Pisani was elected Doge,

the villa was already inhabitable, even if the interior work would continue for some time to come.

The façade on the Naviglio is still redolent of baroque tastes in the Caryatids on the central body holding up the balcony, from which proceed Corynthian semi-columns which in their turn hold up the trabeation and the triangular tympanum crowned with statues. The two wings, punctuated by Ionic lesenes and crowned by parapets with statues, are closed off by the triangular tympana of the lateral bodies. The façade overlooking the garden, even though it has the same volumes as the main façade, presents a cool Neoclassical elegance in the sharp rhythm of the squashed lesenes which stand out against the smooth plaster along the first floor, in sharp contrast with the rustication that covers the ground floor.

After a short break, due to the death of the commissioners and the large amount of money required by the family for such costly work, the villa was resumed by the Doge's son Ermolao I, called Alvise, who had married Giustiniana Pisani, the last descendent and heiress of the wealthy branch of the Santa Maria Zobenigo Pisanis.

This is the phase during which the apartment decorations were completed by, amongst others, Francesco Simonini and Jacopo Guarana. The same is true for the large ballroom, which contains a frescoed architectural structure by Pietro Visconti, around which there runs a sculpted wooden gallery, with monochrome statues painted by Guarana on the friezes over the entrances and windows, while the ceiling contains a frescoed apotheosis of the Pisani family undertaken by Giambattista Tiepolo, assisted by his son Giandomenico, between 1761 and 1762.

Left: the kaffeehaus *on a little knoll surrounded by a ring of water.*

Above: the hexagonal pavilion in the exedra, based on a design by Girolamo Frigimelica.

Below: the richly-decorated gate dividing the flower-bed parterre *from the area dedicated to the greenhouses.*

Left: the ceiling of the ball room in Villa Pisani, with the complex architectural weave by Pietro Visconti, the faux-relief compositions above the gallery, and, in the centre of the ceiling, the Apotheosis of the Pisani Family by Giambattista Tiepolo, 1761-1762.

Below: view of the ball room, Villa Pisani.

Above: the Stanza delle Virtù, with complex frescoed decorations containing 18th-century paintings depicting allegories of the Virtues.

Below: the Sala delle Vedute o dei Giardini, with scenes of villa gardens, attributed by some to Giuseppe Zais and others to Francesco Battaglioli.

Opposite page: Vicereine Amalia's bedroom, with the elegant four-poster bed shaped like a marquee; the room was decorated 1808-1811 when the villa was the residence of Eugène Beauharnais, the Viceroy of Italy.

With the fall of the Republic, Ermolao I, who had already been ambassador to Madrid and Paris during the revolution and procurator of St Mark since 1793, was nominated member of the provisional commune and sent to Paris in 1806 to pay homage to the emperor. In 1807 he sold the Stra property to Napoleon himself, who wanted the villa for Eugène Beauharnais, viceroy of Italy. Beauharnais called on the architects Giovanni Antonio Antolini, Giuseppe Mezzani and Giuseppe Maria Soli to make substantial changes on the villa between 1807 and 1814.

Work was carried out both on the interior (which was restructured according to the needs of the vice royal court, and included the two bathrooms and the redecoration of a great many rooms) and the exterior (the park was extended when Villa Cappello and other land were bought; a great number of tall trees were planted and a series of secondary perspectival views and numerous statues were removed). During the Lombardy-Veneto Reign, Stra maintained its status as official residence. The Austrian emperor's court and other illustrious guests demanded that maintenance work be continually carried out. This came to

a stop in 1866, when the villa became property of the Italian state.

Even though the villa and park were declared national monuments in 1882, the entire complex was inappropriately used. The villa and park were eventually abandoned and, in 1909, it was given over to the University of Padua, who used it as their Institute for Hydrotechnical Research. It was the Institute's research that led to the excavation of a large cement tub between the villa and stables. In 1913 an attempt was made to fill in the excavation with a baroque-like trilobate fixture, decorated with statues and balustrades.

After further disastrous interventions (in 1934 it even hosted the first official meeting between Hitler and Mussolini), the Eastern Veneto Superintendent for the Environment and Architectural Heritage decided, in the 1990s, to begin restoration work on the building. It should be particularly noted that restoration work was also undertaken on the *Vaserie degli agrumi*, a sort of garden-within-the-garden constructed during Beauharnais' stay and extended by the Viceroy Ranieri Habsburg, which boasted an important collection of citrus plants.

Villa Manin

Passariano

Above: view of the villa from the entrance towers.

Opposite page: aerial view of the Passariano complex.

The Manin family, originally from Fiesole, was one of those which, during the clash between Guelfs and Ghibellines, had to abandon Florence in 1279 and moved to Friuli. Careful marriage planning brought Antonio Manin, in 1578, not only a wife in Aloisia di Valvasone, but also her complete dowry, which included land in Sedigliano, from which depended Passariano, a small town in the middle of Friuli. The family that had played such an important role in bringing Friuli under Venetian domination, demonstrated loyalty to the Republic during the Cambrai War

and during the war against Cyprus and Gradisc. They were so loyal, in fact, that in the early 17th century, the Manins were rewarded by being granted seigneurial rights over the county of Polcegno and Fanna, as well as Brugnis, and the awarding of military office.

The social upward mobility was matched by their increased economic clout. In 1651, Lodovico Manin acquired patrician dignity by giving 100,000 ducats to help finance the war against Candia. Whenever land went up for sale, the Manins were among the major buyers, and eventually ended up the largest landowners in the region. After having bought their patrician standing, the family moved to Venice, where they took out a perpetual lease on Palazzo dei Dolfin in San Salvador, overlooking the Grand Canal. The building had been built in 1536 by Jacopo Sansovino; the family bought it in 1787.

The family's patronage of the arts, whereby they financed the decorations for the choir in the Udine duomo and the Gesuiti church in Venice (here they also built a magnificent family chapel in the Scalzi church), aimed also at celebrating the family itself, thus guaranteeing their entry into the

highest echelons of Venice society. The end result was the marriage between Francesco, Lodovico's son, and Elisabetta Foscari, one of the most illustrious of the *case nuove*. The rise of the family reached its highest moment when Lodovico II was elected doge. He was to have the thankless task of handing the Republic over to Napoleon, who, on October 28th 1797, set up his headquarters in Villa Passariano. This is where the Campoformio Treaty was signed, a treaty that sanctioned the fall of the Serenissima and the annexation of the Veneto to Austria.

At Passariano, which was the heart of the overwhelming property owned by the Manins (who held more than 6,000 hectares), Ludovico I began work on a suitable residence. This was in the mid-16th century, just after the family had been granted patrician status. The suggestion for the villa came from Giuseppe Benoni, *proto* of the Palma fortress and later the author of the *dogana da mar* in Venice.

In 1659, Ludovico passed away, and his son Francesco took on the task of continuing work on the villa, which would be completed in the early 18th century and would rival the Contarini complex in Piazzola and the Pisani complex in Stra.

The prime mover behind the project was Domenico Rossi, who was very partial to Palladian schemes and a forerunner in the Veneto of the nascent Neoclassical movement. He was responsible in Venice for the San Stae façade, as well as Palazzo Corner della Regina and the interior of the Gesuiti church, where the Manins had provided funds, as has already been pointed out.

At Passariano, Rossi built a central body with a horizontally marked façade which extends to the two lateral orthogonal porticoed barchesse,

Page 242: the main façade of Villa Passariano, with the attic floor topped by a triangular tympanum which was added after 1745, by Giorgio Massari.

Page 243 below: the large curvilinear barchessa to the west, with one of the two towers.

Page 243 above: façade of the seigneurial chapel the Manin family had built.

Opposite page: the large central tondo on the ceiling in the north-west room, frescoed by Ludovico Dorigny in 1708, and depicting the allegory of the felicity of nature.

Above: details of the north-east room with frescoes by Ludovico Dorigny with monochrome scenes of the Judgement of Paris and Apollo and Daphne.

Below: the villa's central hall.

with pinnacles. The barchesse are followed by large gates leading to the countryside and the spectacular arched hemicycle punctuated by lesenes designed by Piazza Rotonda, divided by Piazza Quadra, behind the villa, by two semi-elliptical fish ponds. This is the most characteristic element of the entire complex, and was obviously inspired by the columned hemicycle in St Peter's Square in Rome.

Two towers, topped off with triangular tympana on all four sides, close off the large exedra looking out onto the countryside over a mixtilinear fish pond, crossed by an arched bridge.

The front of the villa overlooking the garden is delimited by the two wings of outhouses, which are positioned at right angles and flanked by two towered bodies. Later the Manins asked Giorgio Massari to supervise the raising of the central section of the main building by adding an attic with triangular tympanum. This was completed in 1745.

The interiors are heavily indebted to 18th- century interventions in the large central hall on the ground floor, with connecting galleries and rococo framed decorations and stuccoes.

Lodovico Dorigny worked in the villa in 1708, when he put together a series of decorations in one of the ground floor rooms. Here he used every available centimetre of wall space and worked on the ceiling, where he painted the happiness of nature in the large central tondo and Love, Peace, Harmony and Abundance in the lateral gilt oculae.

Mythological statues, alluding to the beguiling power of seduction, and allegories of the seasons and continents (on a gilt mosaic background) are the subjects for the wall decorations; these were structured according to an overwhelming apparatus overflowing with figures, which the commissioning family particularly loved. The same

commissioners were to re-employ Dorigny, who was the only artist (born in Paris and schooled in Rome) able to satisfy the desire for self-exaltation demonstrated by the new patricians in a Venetian context that was devoid of any important figures.

One of the happiest architectural moments in the Passariano complex is the seigneurial chapel, with sculptures by Giuseppe Torretti. It became the church for the entire town, which was organised and conditioned by the compositional scheme of the villa.

Even though impoverished, the statuary undertaken by the Bonazzas and Groppellis in the villa park is remarkable. In 1714 an unknown French architect was brought in to reorganise the garden, which was restructured to reflect the monumentality of Piazza Quadra and Piazza Rotonda. It was filled with caprices and inventions of all sorts, and made enormous use of hydraulic machines and apparatuses. Towards the end of the 18th century, at the same time as restoration work was being carried out on the Venetian *palazzo*, the Manins brought in the architect Giannantonio Selva to transform the formal garden according to new Anglo-Chinese principles.

In 1863 the park was reorganised yet again by the Friuli architect Pietro Quaglia, who enhanced the naturalistic aspect by putting in a large lawn in the shape of a boot in the centre, an obviously patriotic symbol, surrounded by masses of trees and winding paths. In November 1917, Charles I of Habsburg and William II of Germany used the villa to celebrate their victory over the Italian army at Caporetto.

Passariano remained the property of the Manin family until 1962, when it was bought by the state and handed over to the Ente per le Ville Venete. In 1969 it was given to the Friuli Venezia Giulia Region, who turned it into a museum and cultural centre.

Villa Marcello

Levada

Above: the rear façade of Villa Marcello.

Opposite page: the main Neopalladian prospect with porticoed terraces linking the lateral barchesse to the villa.

In the plains north of Padua, which were settled as early as the Palaeo-Veneto period and "centurionised" during the reign of Augustus, there was a vast influx of patrician Venetian settlements during the Serenissima.

At Levada di Piombino Dese, bordering on lands owned by the Corner family, are the lands belonging to the Marcellos, a *famiglia nova*, with a Doge to their credit and who claimed to descend, according to an imaginative family tree, from Claudius Marcellus, a general in the Second Punic War, who fought against Hannibal.

The most famous family member is in fact Benedetto, a member of the Quarantia and procurator in Pola, a respected musician who published a collection of fifty psalms entitled *Estro poetico armonico* in 1724. His fame also rests on a satirical essay, "Il teatro alla moda" (1720), which criticises the widespread immorality in the musical theatre of the period.

The Marcellos had been in Levada since the 16th century; they were responsible for much of the irrigation scheme in the territory, with its vast water supply, and the construction of a traditional Venetian villa preceded by two porticoed *barchesse* at right angles to

Left: the Italian garden, Villa Marcello.

Belowe, left: the villa's fish pond.
Right: the octagonal tower.

the villa's main axis. The Levada estate was passed on through marriage to the Corners and Morosinis, and then to the Maruzzis, a family of bankers from Epirus.

In the early 19th century, Alessandrina Maruzzi brought the estate as dowry to Count Sumarakov, an aide-de-camp for the Russian Zar, who then lost the villa and land gambling to the Hungarian count Helicaj, who then put it up for sale. N H Girolamo Marcello bought the estate, and thus brought Levada back into the family,

who still own it and jealously guard it. It is, in fact, one of the few residences that has maintained most of its original furnishing, which goes back mostly to the 18th-century, an era in which the Levada villa was radically restructured and assumed its current neo-Palladian form with the imposing Ionic semi-column façade over a delicately rusticated podium, linked, via a porticoed terrace, to the large lateral *barchesse*. Triangular tympana over the window openings on the *piano nobile*, all with restrained balustrade balconies, and a triangular fronton crowned by Classical effigies, the central one of which is a representation

Opposite page: view of the piano nobile hall,
with 18th-century stucco decorations.
The fresco painted 1750-1755 by Giambattista
Crosato depicts Alexander the Great showing mercy
and clemency to the family of Darius.

Above: bedroom on the piano nobile,
with elaborate rococo stucco decorations.

of Claudius Marcellus, complete the main façade. The secondary façade overlooking the park is, however, redolent of 16th-century tastes. In the area behind the complex, closed in by the villa and farm houses, there is a formal Italian garden subdivided into four large flower-beds with a central mixtilinear pool with fountain and statues of marine divinities. The garden also contains statues of the seasons, statues in "Ancient" garb on the monumental pilasters of the main entrance gates, and a series of dwarves near the fish pond. The 19th-century English garden is also noteworthy, and extends for seven hectares around the villa.

Equally worthy of note is the broad cypress-lined avenue which leads into the country from the trench just beyond the wrought iron entrance gate, and the hornbeam-lined avenues alongside the rectangular fish pond behind the villa (the pond was originally the result of excavations of sand and earth used in building the complex).

In the eastern sector of the park there is an aviary dating back to the 16th century. It is octagonal in shape, and contains the remains of 18th-century decorations and landscapes.

The interior of the villa maintains the traditional tripartite villa layout with beamed ceilings and Venetian flooring. The *portego de mezo* on the ground floor is eminently 16th-century in the simple elegance of the space and monumental

doorways topped by triangular tympanum, while the side staircases show obvious signs of the 18th-century restoration in the rococo decorations in the frames and in the marble fireplaces whose internal area is covered with Delft majolica tiles.

Rococo, however, triumphs on the *piano nobile*, with the stucco decorations over the doorways and windows, the frames painted onto the walls, and the large polychromatic stucco landscapes in the rooms over cartoons by Giuseppe Zais, an appreciated Belluno landscape artist.

The ballroom is theatrically impressive. It takes its height from the *piano nobile* and the upper mezzanine floor, along which there is a sinuously-structured gallery with faux marble wooden balustrades. Giovanni Battista Crosato, a late-17th-century early-18th-century Venetian artist who had worked as a set designer and fresco artist at the Savoy court in Turin, was called to the villa by the Maruzzis in 1750-1755. When he returned to Venice in 1736, Crosato painted the large vault in the Ca' Rezzonico ballroom on the Grand Canal; he then worked for the Pisanis at Stra, and then the Marcellos in Levada, just before his death in 1758.

The fundamental elements in the decorative layout in the Levada ballroom are the precious gilt stucco surrounds for the frescoes on the walls (the idea was to simulate four separate paintings with frames) and the celestial backdrop representing Olympus on the ceiling. The wall scenes are based on episodes from the life of Alexander the Great, one of the most popular subjects for commissioners in that period, mainly because the great leader was seen to bring together noble virtues as well as magnanimity and generosity.

Crosato's spectacular virtuosity, his lively chromaticism and his realistic representation of detail, though a cut below the absolute mastery of Tiepolo, make the Levada cycle an extremely important artistic work.

But it is the details in Villa Marcello that also add to its characteristic atmosphere: the windows themselves, which still include hand-blown panes of glass with lead seals; the walnut doors with their original doorknobs; the Murano glass chandeliers, some of which are extremely inventive; the furniture itself, some of which, such as the furniture in the ballroom, was made especially for the house.

Villa Trissino

Trissino

Above: aerial view of the upper villa, Trissino, with, in the foreground, landscape showing the citrus garden and the terraced stables.

Below: aerial view of the lower villa with large garden terrace with central octagonal pool.

Opposite page: the oldest nucleus of the Trissino complex in Trissino, which was part of the old castle which the Venetians had demolished.

Trissino lies in the middle valley of the Agno, to the north-east of Vicenza. The old town is built on the slopes of a knoll, and takes its name from the family who were the feudal lords over most of the valley - the Trissinos. Noblemen of Frankish origins who had a castle in the area which dominated the low-lying land from Ghisa to Cornedo, the Trissinos managed to maintain their rank and position even after subjugation to Venice. Gian Giorgio Trissino, a humanist and diplomat, was mentor to Andrea di Pietro della Gondola, whom he renamed "the Palladio".

The ancient castle of Trissino, demolished by order of the Venetians, was transformed into a residence in successive phases. The first of these dates back to 1484 and 1493, as can be evinced from the dates on a well-head and memorial tablet. The entrance doorway from the piazza in front of the church then gives the year 1593. But the radical changes, which were to leave their mark in the structuring of the entire estate, were carried out from 1722 by the Lugano architect Francesco Muttoni.

When Muttoni died in 1747, Marcantonio Trissino called in his cousin, Girolamo Dal Pozzo, to complete the work. From a noble Verona family, Dal Pozzo studied with his uncle, Count Alessandro Pompei, who had designed numerous public and private buildings in Verona. The end result is an elongated building, set at right angles to an older building, which was perhaps the old keep. The main façade, which only just juts out in the middle section rounded off by an attic surmounted by statues, faces onto a courtyard, enclosed on its two minor sides within a wall that allows access to the garden through arched openings. There is a balustrade along the *piano nobile* of the façade which continues right up to the hanging terrace of the *cavallerizza*. The ground floor openings have quoins. Above these there is a string of small windows along the mezzanine and then other windows along the *piano nobile* with alternating triangular and arched tympana, except for the central run which is entirely arched. While work was underway on this "upper villa" which belonged to the Trissino Baston family, the other branch of the family, the Trissino Riales, began work on their "lower villa". Nothing is known about the architect involved in the villa, not only because of a lack of documentary evidence, but also because of the exhaustive restoration undertaken by Count Alessandro Trissino in 1841. The building, in fact, had virtually been destroyed by lightning, and a later fire led to the house being abandoned and allowed to decline.

There are therefore two Trissino villas, positioned in such a way that they define the entire urban layout of the hill, with courtyards and gardens adapted to the orographic situation of the site.

Page 256-257: the long 18th-century façade
of the upper villa built by the Trissino Baston
branch of the family according to a project by the
Veronese Girolamo dal Pozzo.

Opposite page: façade of the lower villa which
belonged to the Trissino Riale branch of the family,
and left to crumble after a fire caused by lightning.

Below: allegorical statues along the wall
surrounding the secret garden to the east of the
upper villa.

Francesco Muttoni was surely responsible, according to the design documents, for the garden of the "upper villa", for the two parallel rectilinear walkways in the hill, placed at different heights and leading to an octagonal belvedere and to a no longer extant flower garden. The composition's salient element is the octagonal belvedere, with stone cordons demarcating the outline of the *parterres* that crown the central motif, which is also octagonal in form. The "lower villa", with its characteristic crenellated lateral bodies, dominates from a rectangular land terrace over a large quadrangular terraced lawn, with at its centre an octagonal water basin with statues on the high podiums placed at the edges.

The staircases linking the two floors and the belvedere below (on a third level) are spectacular. Stone balustrades, broken up by extremely detailed statues, delimit the entire space. The geometrical figure and the positioning and proportions demonstrate the evident intention of making the upper belvedere and the lower basin two identical reference points in the overall organisation of the park.

In the early 19th century the Riale and Trissino Baston properties were united by the latter branch, who commissioned

Left: detail of the small minaret tower of the stables.

Right: the monumental entrance gates to the garden, lower villa, with twinned and single columns crowned by elaborate heraldic motifs.

Opposite page: detail of the octagonal pool in the terraced garden, lower villa.

the Vicentine architect Otton Calderari to come up with a project for the restructuring of the park (the project was never completed, as Calderari died in 1803). Calderari intended to eliminate the remains of the wild woods, which the Muttonis and Dal Pozzos had kept, to make room for a complex ensemble of steps and terraces. In the years to come, however, pride of place was given to the landscape qualities of the park with the introduction of high-growing trees and rare species, as well as winding pathways. A "garden of the dead" was also created, which included steles and memorial stones strewn about the underbrush. A separate chapter should be devoted to the monumental wrought iron entranceways which are impressive because of their imaginative and innovative nature. The connection between courtyard and pathway to the belvedere, in fact, is constituted by a series of pilasters, decorated with pinnacles, and forming an exedra. The entrance to the "lower villa", with its twinned and single columns crowned by elaborate heraldic motifs and interspersed with large windows with curvilinear tympanum surmounted by decorative vases, is still rather complex and monumental.

The vast sculptural collection in the Trissino garden also plays a very important role in the organisation of the spatial dimension, alluding to a connection between the architect's idea and the work of the sculptor, who was most probably Orazio Marinali and his workshop. There are two fundamental aspects to the sculptures. One is the use of mythological statues in the path leading to the belvedere; the other is constituted by the vast repertory of statues along the terraces of the "villa below", formed by a group of farm workers, hunters and musicians, who look down towards the "theatre of the world" in the lower *parterre*, where there are the allegories of continents, the seasons and the character of man. There are four more statues of the seasons in the secret garden, to the east of the "upper villa". Tommaso and Andrea Porta from Verona worked on the interiors of the "upper villa", providing a decorative cycle with landscape themes, among which there is a very interesting view of Trissino with a clear view of the two villas in their natural context. The Trissino complex, after having been inherited by the da Porto counts, now belongs to the Marzotto family.

Left: detail of the long arras gallery in the upper villa, Trissino.

Below: detail of the panoramic view of Trissino frescoed in one of the ground-floor corridors, upper villa, by the Veronese artists Tommaso and Andrea Porta, 1765.

La Musella

San Martino Buon Albergo

Verona's suburbs stretch out to the east towards the foothills that make up the extremities of the Lessini hills. There, in the industrial suburb of San Martino Buon Albergo, organised linearly along the state road that links Verona and Vicenza, there is along the side of an octagonal temple a monumental entrance to the Musella estate, which covers 367 hectares, 30 of which are parkland and 120 of which are woodland, and which until a few years ago constituted one single property.

A row of plane trees flanks the road that leads to the estate, which becomes a majestic alley of cypresses in the bit that slopes steeply up the hill, on which there is the main complex.

The original settlement harks back to the early 16th century, when, with the name of *corte delle colombare*, it belonged to the Marioni family, gold merchants from Caravaggio (Bergamo) who had moved to Verona in the second half of the 15th century. In 1607, the *corte delle colombare* and its adjoining land, was sold to the Muselli family, who eventually gave their name to the house. The Musellis, from Torri del Benaco, had moved to Verona in about the mid-15th century as hatters and then wool, linen and silk merchants. During the 17th and 18th centuries, the family continued to invest its profits in farms, houses and shops in the city and the country. After the 1630 Plague, the family made great financial efforts to buy the noble titles that would allow them to join the city's noble council.

When they finally attained aristocratic status in the mid-17th century, they moved from the old houses in Santa Maria Antica to a new *palazzo* in Corso Castelvecchio, built alongside the Sanmicheli home of the Canossas and by the transformation, between 1654 and 1709, of the old *corte delle colombare* into a suitably noble residence. Even the purchase of works of art and archaeological finds was part of the family's plan, so much so that Giacomo Muselli managed to put together a rather large art collection including paintings by Giorgione, Titian, Tintoretto, Veronese, Correggio and Sebastiano del Piombo, which was sold off in 1671 by his heirs to the regent of France.

During the 18th century, the Musellis were also to the forefront of the literary milieu, with Francesco, a prefect at the Biblioteca Capitolare, and Jacopo, who published a work on his own rare coin collection in 1752. The book was dedicated to Federick Christian of Poland, which eventually landed him the concession of the title of marquis.

The Musella, with constant additions of adjoining land and other rural houses and courtyards, was held by the Musellis until 1861, when Matilde Muselli was forced to sell because of bad debts run up by her

Above: detail of the western façade, with the sequence of statues of Caesar on elevated hanging podia.

Below: overall view of the western façade, punctuated by two-light windows and the statues of Caesar.

Left: the many-lobed fish pond in the terraced garden, with, in the background, the southern façade of the villa, which was restored according to Moorish tastes by Giacomo Franco, post-mid-19th century.

husband, Giangirolamo Orti Manara, to the banker Luigi Trezza, who was later ennobled by the emperor Franz Joseph.

The estate was further extended with other purchases both by Luigi Trezza and his son Cesare, who inherited the Musella in 1870. Maddalena Trezza di Musella, Cesare's only heir, married the count, later duke, Pietro d'Acquarone in 1922. He was the last minister for the Royal Family of Italy, and his descendents inherited the estate of San Martino Buon Albergo.

*Opposite page: the villa library
with vaulted ceiling with faux-balustrade
and putti.*

*Below: the central hall in the oldest nucleus
of the Musella, with ceiling frescoed
1686-1687 by the Veronese Biagio Falcieri,
with central wind rose which gives
its name to the room.*

The Musella villa is now the end result of a series of interventions that date from the early 16th century to the 1930s and, as far as the park is concerned, to the post-war period.

The monumental entrance, which is at the end of a long row of cypresses, bears the date 1709 on one of the pillars and opens onto the grotto-nymphaeum beneath the large terraced garden that precedes the Moorish southern façade of the villa. In fact, the work that has been undertaken over the centuries has transformed the Musella into a quadrilateral building, with a central courtyard and four different façades, disposed according to the four cardinal points.

The intervention which has left the greatest mark was undertaken in 1859 on behalf of Matilde Muselli by Giacomo Franco. This work continued until 1861-2, when the property was passed on to Luigi Trezza.

Giacomo Franco, of noble birth, had married Antonietta Vela, Matilde Muselli's niece. A self-taught man with a passion for drawing, he was made professor at the Accademia di Pittura e Scultura in Verona at the age of 23. A regular traveller, he frequented the Paduan circle of Camillo Boito and Pietro Selvatico, working in the rich sphere of stylistic contaminations which goes under the heading of Eclecticism, with forms that oscillate between Neoclassicism, Neogothic and Moorish.

Well versed through birth and marriage in the high Veneto society of the period, he used his Eclecticism to restore numerous Verona villas. The language chosen for the Musella goes from the Renaissance of the western façade, punctuated on the *piano nobile* by seven large two-light windows surmounted by floral reliefs and closed off by fretworked stone parapets, accompanied by statues of the twelve Caesars placed on shelves in Gothic style, to the Neogothic of the campanile of the 17th-century seigneurial chapel. There are also Romanesque elements on the façade of chapel itself, and Islamic elements on the southern façade that the eastern façade was supposed to lean against but which was replaced in the late 19th-century by a classically-styled porticoed body. In the southern room, which corresponds to the main part of the old house, Franco used the classical scheme which the Musellis had already defined, and limited himself to adding along the side sectors two niches with the statues of

Right: detail of the room linking the reception hall and the bedrooms, where there are evident late-19th century interventions inspired by French Neo-rococo.

Opposite page: view of one of the corridors running around the terraced cloister, decorated with rococo stuccoes.

Diana and Demeter. This wing, with its traditional Venetian plan, contains the rooms frescoed by Biagio Falcieri (from 1686), who was also responsible for the chapel decorations. This is a rich and imaginative framing apparatus that is played out in the pavilion ceilings of the passage hall and the side rooms. The most original part is the wind rose, painted in the little elliptical cupola in the centre of the pavilion ceiling in the passage hall. The work carried out between 1927 and 1939 by the Duchess Maddalena d'Acquarone includes an internal courtyard which has been transformed into a terraced cloister with fountain, enclosed by windows and decorated with rococo stuccoes along the corridors. Even the dining room and the staircase leading to the mezzanine floors have something of the International style of the period,

and are obviously inspired by the French 18th century.

The garden was restructured in the 17th- century, but all that remains are the terraces, the grotto, the mixtilinear fishing pond, part of the sculptural works and the large aviary, traditionally attributed to Sanmicheli. This is a quadrangular pavilion with large cupola formed by an iron grid, covered by nets and with a hypostyle courtyard, where the Doric trabeation with triglyphs and metopes is surmounted by the heraldic symbols of the Trissino family: plait, wheel, tower and eagle. This was added in the 19th century by order of the Trezzas.

The large landscape park, however, dates back to a restructuring commissioned by Cesare Trezza between 1882 and 1884, when thousands of cubic metres of earth were moved to construct lawns, ponds, small lakes, little waterfalls and streams. This was supervised by the engineer Ettore Paladini in terms of the irrigation scheme (which includes the impressive Perlar cistern containing 700,000 litres of water), and by Gerolamo Zanoni in terms of the layout, inspired by the Villa Reale park in Monza. In those years a large glass and steel greenhouse was built for the cultivation of orchids, and exotic species such as the dwarf palm were introduced. In the 1950s, the English landscapist Russell Page restructured the terraced garden to the south, partly replacing the gravel with lawn, and building a large rectangular pool which was then transformed into a swimming pool.

Villa Rizzardi Guerrieri

Pojega

Above: the cypress path that leads to the so-called belvedere, one of the caprices planned by the Veronese Luigi Trezza to decorate the villa garden.

Opposite page: the main façade, designed according to Neo-Renaissance tastes by Filippo Messedaglia, 1868-1870. The modern sculptures are by Miguel Berrocal.

In the plain that extends from the walled city of Monselice towards Conselve, Giovanni Francesco Tassello decided to build a villa on the estate he owned, where he had already found a preceding rural building used as a storehouse and depot. The model chosen for the residence was the 16th-century model of an almost perfectly cubic building, with a four-pitched roof, the ground floor reserved for servants, a *piano nobile* and granaries, according to the Venetian *fondaco* house, with a central passage hall. The openings, which are laid out according to a rigid scheme, are all architraved except for the central opening on the *piano nobile*, which has a small wrought iron balcony with vertical parapet, flanked by two windows so as to almost form a Serlian. Four string-courses run the length of the entire building and constitute the only decorative element along with the two tall tower-like chimneys on the roof.

Tassello had done nothing other than conform to an archetype with many examples in the vicinity, such as Villa Corner in Costa Calcinara, Villa Renier in Monticelli and the villa built by Francesco Duodo and designed by Vincenzo Scamozzi on the Rocca di Monselice in the late 16th century. Unlike these, however, Tassello's villa was to be given an external staircase (which was never built) with one, or perhaps even two, flights, that would have led to the *piano nobile* from the courtyard in front of the house, which also contained a small yard in terracotta and the old barchesse.

The project was interrupted almost certainly because Giovanni Francesco died of the plague in 1630 along with his only son Gaetano. Tassello, feeling the end was nigh, had written a will in which he bequeathed his estate to the community of Monselice, where he was the town doctor, so that any profits could be used for the poor. From that moment on the Palazzetto was used as a farm by peasants who would rent it, and who covered the frescoes with whitewash in the main rooms. The villa thus remained unchanged for years, lost among the cereal crops, until the property was

Opposite page: the exedra rounding off the secret garden, with at its centre a statue dedicated to a river deity.

Left: detail of the open-air theatre.

Right: interior of a small circular rustic temple; below: detail of the Italian garden which leads to the hornbeam gallery.

put up for auction in 1917, where it was bought by the Businaro family from Monselice, who were mainly interested in the farming land of the estate. Towards the end of the 1960s, Aldo, the grandson of the 1917 buyer, bought his brothers out and intended to refurbish the villa. By sheer chance, Aldo Businari met Carlo Scarpa (1906-1978), one of the greatest 20th-century Italian architects, in Japan at a design exhibition.

It was therefore because of this unique relationship between architect and commissioner, according to the best traditions, that the die was cast and led to a series of interventions that were to last from 1971 until Scarpa's accidental death. The villa is thus the

end result not so much of a unitary project, but a gradual accretion of logical ideas and associations that mainly impinged on the space surrounding the villa.

Scarpa brought his passion to bear on this minor example of aulic architecture, and included the façade in his plans to renovate the building. He wanted to reintroduce the external entrance staircase, but it was never to be realised. He limited himself to emphasising the chimney pots, purposefully different in typology (the one on the right is tuba-shaped, as are the Venetian chimney pots that can be seen from Carpaccio on).

Scarpa's ability to recontextualise historical buildings by forcefully impressing his own vision has led to an admirable integration of environment and landscape. The first intervention, in 1971, dealt with the articulation of the entrance to the villa and the construction of the enclosing wall. This was followed in 1973 by the berceau, an open space, delimited by concrete walls, covered by vines, collocated among tall trees behind the villa, just along an enclosing wall, with an exit onto the countryside. There, a double row of cypress trees defines a path that runs parallel to the enclosing wall, according to indications given by Scarpa himself. Even the space behind the back façade was reorganised by Scarpa, who originally planned to restructure the ground floor entrance to the villa. What really got the critics going, however, was what he did with the front courtyard, which is the first thing any visitor sees. Here he used traditional red bricks to put together a raised surface, the end result of the intersection of two different planes that converge on two points called *sun* and *moon*.

The space therefore becomes at the

Opposite page: the central hall furnished according to the tastes of the artist Miguel Berrocal.

Above: a detailed view of the internal staircase.

Center: view of the central hall.

Below: detailed view of the dining room.

same time a reception space, as the entrance to the villa proper (in fact this is where the external staircase to the *piano nobile* was supposed to be), and a functional place, as it also had to be used to stack up the various farming goods produced by the farm. Before he died, Scarpa also worked on a project for the restructuring of the rustic building, built by Businaro in the early 20th century at right angles to the house and the old barchessa. The architect opened it up with a central breach from which the most important view is directly onto the courtyard, and masking the garage on the right with a sliding doorway with vivacious background – these were realised after his death, and based on the designs he left behind. The villa interiors are worth mentioning where the frescoed decorations, painted before 1627, have been restored. In the passage hall the long walls are divided up by faux ochre columns placed on a faux marble podium which delimit large spaces probably destined for canvases; while the central doors are decorated with copies of painted winged victories. Above, under the beams, there is a frieze depicting episodes from the *Aeneid* within elaborate frames. In the middle room, towards the west, between the two lateral rooms, the frieze, animated by fake caryatids, depicts the signs of the zodiac, within the evident confines of the surrounds. The villa décor is also remarkable. It was put together by the owners themselves, and contains contemporary art collections and designer furniture, some of which was made by Scarpa himself.

Il Palazzetto

Monselice

Above: the old outhouse of the villa.

Opposite page: the main façade of the Palazzetto, with large fireplaces designed by Carlo Scarpa and, in the foreground, the front "yard" with traditional red bricks on a raised surface.

In the plain that extends from the walled city of Monselice towards Conselve, Giovanni Francesco Tassello decided to build a villa on the estate he owned, where he had already found a preceding rural building used as a storehouse and depot. The model chosen for the residence was the 16th-century model of an almost perfectly cubic building, with a four-pitched roof, the ground floor reserved for servants, a *piano nobile* and granaries, according to the Venetian *fondaco* house, with a central passage hall. The openings, which are laid out according to a rigid scheme, are all architraved except for the central opening on the *piano nobile*, which has a small wrought iron balcony with vertical parapet, flanked by two windows so as to almost form a Serlian. Four string-courses run the length of the entire building and constitute the only decorative element along with the two tall tower-like chimneys on the roof.

Tassello had done nothing other than conform to an archetype with many examples in the vicinity, such as Villa Corner in Costa Calcinara, Villa Renier in Monticelli and the villa built by Francesco Duodo and designed by Vincenzo Scamozzi on the Rocca di Monselice in the late 16th century. Unlike these, however, Tassello's villa was to be given an external staircase (which was never built) with one, or perhaps even two, flights, that would have led to the *piano nobile* from the courtyard in front of the house, which also contained a small yard in terracotta and the old barchesse.

The project was interrupted almost certainly because Giovanni Francesco died of the plague in 1630 along with his only son Gaetano. Tassello, feeling the end was nigh, had written a will in which he bequeathed his estate to the community of Monselice, where he was the town doctor, so that any profits could be used for the poor. From that moment on the Palazzetto was used as a farm by peasants who would rent it, and who covered the frescoes with whitewash in the main rooms. The villa thus remained unchanged for years, lost among the cereal crops, until the property was put up for auction in 1917, where it was bought by the Businaro family

Opposite page: the rear façade of the villa.

Above: detailed view of the berceau, made in 1973 using concrete structures covered with vines.

Below: the sliding garage door with vividly-coloured sections, by Carlo Scarpa.

from Monselice, who were mainly interested in the farming land of the estate. Towards the end of the 1960s, Aldo, the grandson of the 1917 buyer, bought his brothers out and intended to refurbish the villa. By sheer chance, Aldo Businari met Carlo Scarpa (1906-1978), one of the greatest 20th-century Italian architects, in Japan at a design exhibition.

It was therefore because of this unique relationship between architect and commissioner, according to the best traditions, that the die was cast and led to a series of interventions that were to last from 1971 until Scarpa's accidental death. The villa is thus the end result not so much of a unitary project, but a gradual accretion of logical ideas and associations that mainly impinged on the space surrounding the villa.

Scarpa brought his passion to bear on this minor example of aulic architecture, and included the façade in his plans to renovate the building. He wanted to reintroduce the external entrance staircase, but it was never to be realised. He limited himself to emphasising the chimney pots, purposefully different in typology (the one on the right is tuba-shaped, as are the Venetian chimney pots that can be seen from Carpaccio on).

Scarpa's ability to recontextualise historical buildings by forcefully impressing his own vision has led to an admirable integration of environment and landscape. The first intervention, in 1971, dealt with the articulation of the entrance to the villa and the construction of the enclosing wall. This was followed in 1973 by the berceau, an open space, delimited by concrete walls, covered by vines, collocated among tall trees behind the villa, just along an enclosing wall, with an exit onto the countryside. There, a

double row of cypress trees defines a path that runs parallel to the enclosing wall, according to indications given by Scarpa himself. Even the space behind the back façade was reorganised by Scarpa, who originally planned to restructure the ground floor entrance to the villa. What really got the critics going, however, was what he did with the front courtyard, which is the first thing any visitor sees. Here he used traditional red bricks to put together a raised surface, the end result of the intersection of two different planes that converge on two points called *sun* and *moon*.

The space therefore becomes at the same time a reception space, as the entrance to the villa proper (in fact this is where the external staircase to the *piano nobile* was supposed to be), and a functional place, as it also had to be used to stack up the various farming goods produced by the farm.

Before he died, Scarpa also worked on a project for the restructuring of the rustic building, built by Businaro in the early 20th century at right angles to the house and the old barchessa. The architect opened it up with a central breach from which the most important view is directly onto the courtyard, and masking the garage on the right with a sliding doorway with vivacious background – these were realised after his death, and based on the designs he left behind. The villa interiors are worth mentioning where the frescoed decorations, painted before 1627, have been restored. In the passage hall the long walls are divided up by faux ochre columns placed on a faux marble podium which delimit large spaces probably destined for canvases; while the central doors are decorated with copies of painted winged victories. Above, under the beams, there is a frieze depicting episodes from the *Aeneid* within elaborate frames. In the middle room, towards the west, between the two lateral rooms, the frieze, animated by fake caryatids, depicts the signs of the zodiac, within the evident confines of the surrounds. The villa décor is also remarkable. It was put together by the owners themselves, and contains contemporary art collections and designer furniture, some of which was made by Scarpa himself.

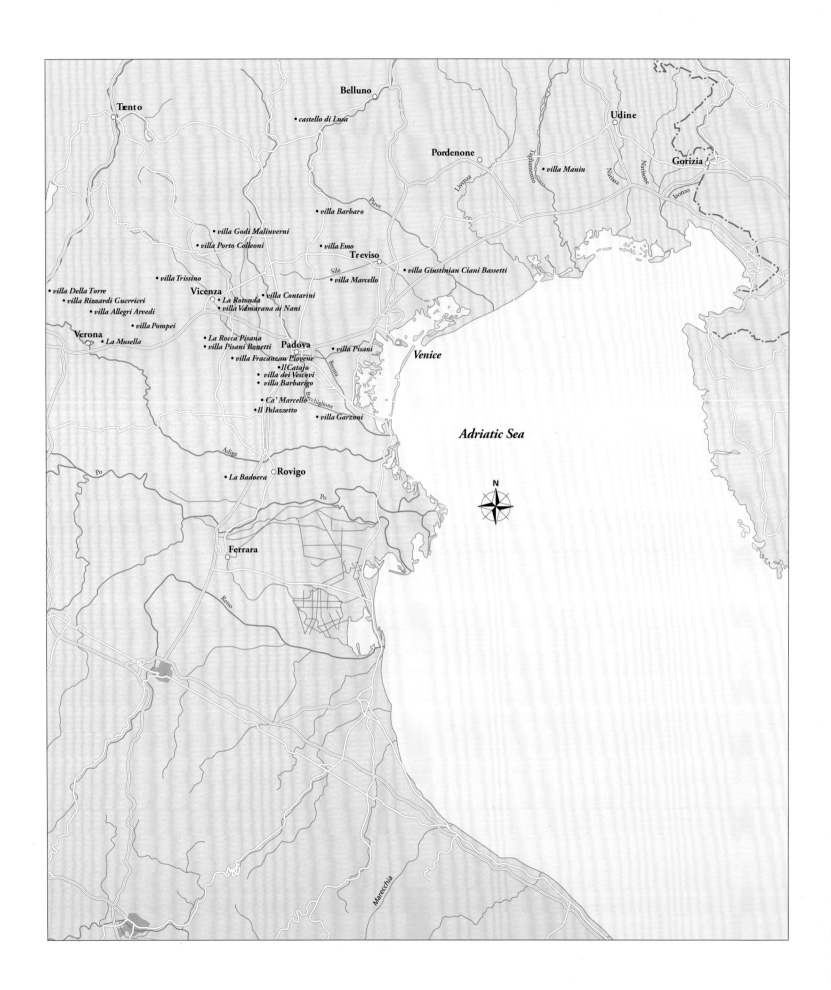

Belluno

• castello di Lusa

Trento

Udine

Pordenone

Gorizia

• villa Manin

• villa Barbaro

• villa Godi Malinverni

• villa Porto Colleoni

• villa Emo

Treviso

• villa Giustinian Ciani Bassetti

Sile

• villa Marcello

• villa Trissino

• villa Della Torre

Vicenza

• La Rotonda

• villa Contarini

• villa Rizzardi Guerrieri

• villa Valmarana ai Nani

• villa Allegri Arvedi

• villa Pompei

Verona

• La Rocca Pisana

Padova

• villa Pisani

• La Musella

• villa Pisani Bonetti

• villa Fracanzan Piovene

Venice

• Il Catajo

• villa dei Vescovi

• villa Barbarigo

Brenta

• Ca' Marcello

Bacchiglione

• Il Palazzetto

• villa Garzoni

Adriatic Sea

Adige

Po

• La Badoera

Rovigo

Po

N

Ferrara

Reno

Marecchia

Bibliography

General Bibliography

Andrea Palladio e la villa Veneta da Petrarca a Carlo Scarpa, a cura di G. Beltramini e H. Burns, Venezia 2005

Palladio, a cura di G. Beltramini e H. Burns, Venezia 2008

Ackerman James Stokes, *La villa. Forma e ideologia*, Torino 1992.

Gli affreschi nelle Ville Venete dal Seicento all'Ottocento, a cura di F. D'Arcais, F. Zava Boccazzi, G. Pavanello, Venezia 1978.

Gli affreschi nelle Ville Venete. Il Cinquecento, a cura di G. Pavanello, V. Mancini, Venezia 2008.

Gli affreschi nelle Ville Venete. Il Seicento, a cura di G. Pavanello, V. Mancini, Venezia 2009.

Gli affreschi nelle Ville Venete. Il Settecento, tomo I e tomo II, a cura di G. Pavanello, Venezia 2010 e 2011.

Alpago Novello Adriano, *Ville della provincia di Belluno*, Milano 1968.

Azzi Visentini Margherita, *La villa in Italia*. Quattrocento e Cinquecento, Milano 1985.

Baldan Alessandro, *Storia della Riviera del Brenta*, Cassola 1978-1982.

Baldan Alessandro, *Ville Venete in territorio padovano e nella Serenissima Repubblica: documentazione, iconografia, testimonianze*, Abano Terme 1986.

Balzaretti Liliana, *Ville Venete*, Milano 1965.

Bassi Elena, *Ville della provincia di Venezia*, Milano 1987.

Beltrami Daniele, *Saggio di storia dell'agricoltura veneta nella Repubblica di Venezia durante l'età moderna*, Venezia 1955.

Beltrami Daniele, *La penetrazione economica dei Veneziani in terraferma. Forza di lavoro e proprietà fondiarie nelle campagne venete dei secoli XVII e XVIII*, Venezia 1961.

Bodefeld Gerda, Hinz Berthold, *Ville Venete*, Milano, 1990.

Brunelli Bruno, Callegari Adolfo, *Ville del Brenta e degli Euganei*, Milano 1931.

Brusatin Manlio, *Venezia nel Settecento: stato, architettura, territorio*, Torino 1980.

Canova Antonio, *Ville del Polesine*, Rovigo 1970.

Cevese Renato, *Ville della provincia di Vicenza*, Milano 1982.

Chiovaro Simonetta, *Le ville nel paesaggio prealpino della provincia di Belluno*, Milano 1997.

Crosato Luciana, *Gli affreschi nelle Ville Venete del Cinquecento*, Treviso 1962.

La cultura della villa. Il Friuli occidentale e Venezia nel Settecento, a cura di U. Trame, Pordenone 1988.

Gaspari Paolo, *Terra patrizia. Aristocrazie terriere e società rurali in Veneto e Friuli: patrizi veneziani, nobili e borghesi nella formazione dell'etica civile delle élite (1797-1920)*, Udine 1993.

Il giardino veneto. Storia e conservazione, a cura di M. Azzi Visentini, Milano 1988.

Kubelik Martin, *Die Villa im Veneto. Zur typologischen Entwicklung im Quattrocento*, München 1977.

Lauritzen Peter, *Ville venete*, Milano 1987.

Mazzotti Giuseppe, *Ville venete*, Treviso 2000.

Muraro Michelangelo, *Civiltà delle ville Venete*, Udine 1986.

Muraro Michelangelo, *Civiltà delle ville Venete*, Venezia 2000.

Prà Antonio, Banchieri Andrea, *Dal castello medioevale alla cultura della villa veneta*, Venezia 1999.

Precerutti Garberi Mercedes, *Affreschi settecenteschi delle Ville Venete*, Milano 1968.

Puppi Lionello, *Andrea Palladio*, Milano 1999.

Sabbadini Roberto, *L'acquisto della tradizione. Aristocrazia tradizione aristocratica e nuova nobiltà a Venezia*, Udine 1995.

Scarpari Gianfranco, *Le ville venete. Dalle mirabili architetture del Palladio alle grandiose dimore del Settecento: un itinerario affascinante e suggestivo nel "verde" di una terra ricca di antiche tradizioni*, Roma 1980.

Semenzato Camillo, *Le ville del Polesine*, Vicenza 1975.

Tiozzo Glauco Benito, *Le ville del Brenta da Lizza, Fusina alla città di Padova*, Venezia 1977.

Ulmer Christoph, *Ville friulane. Storia e civiltà*, Udine 1993.

Venturini Giuseppe, *Il Terraglio e le sue ville*, Mogliano Veneto 1977.

La villa nel veronese, a cura di G. F. Viviani, Verona 1975.

Le ville venete, a cura di G. Mazzotti, Treviso 1987.

Ville venete: catalogo e atlante del Veneto, a cura di A. Padoan, S. Pratali Maffei, D. Dalpozzo, L. Mavian, Venezia 1996.

Ville venete: la Provincia di Padova, a cura di N. Zucchello, Venezia 2001.

Ville venete: la Provincia di Rovigo. Insediamenti nel Polesine, a cur di B. Gabbiani, Venezia 2000.

Ville venete: la Provincia di Treviso, a cura di S. Chiovaro, Venezia 2001.

Ville venete: la Provincia di Verona, a cura di S. Ferrari, Venezia 2003.

Ville Venete: La Provincia di Vicenza, a cura di D. Battilotti, Venezia 2005

Ville Venete: La Provincia di Venezia, a cura di A. Torsello, L. Caselli, Venezia 2005

Ville Venete: La Provincia di Belluno, a cura di S. Chiovaro, Venezia 2004

Ville Venete: La Regione Friuli Venezia Giulia, a cura di S. Pratali Maffei, Venezia 2005

Viviani Giuseppe Franco, Ville della Valpolicella, Verona 1983.

Zorzi Giangiorgio, Le ville e i teatri di Andrea Palladio, Vicenza 1969.

Bibliographical suggestion on specific villas:

Barbantini Nino, *Il castello di Monselice*, Venezia 1940.

Barbieri Franco, *La Rocca Pisana di Vincenzo Scamozzi*, Vicenza 1985.

Bordignon Favero Giampaolo, *La villa Emo di Fanzolo*, Vicenza 1970.

Botter Mario, *La villa Giustinian di Roncade*, Treviso 1955.

Chiappini di Sorio Ileana, Ferri de Lazara Cornelia, *Villa Pisani a Bagnolo di Lonigo*, Milano 1996.

Fontana Loris, *Valsanzibio*, Cittadella 1990.

Il Castello del Cataio, Battaglia Terme, Padova 1994.

Mazzi Bruno, *La villa Godi Valmarana*, Milano 1976.

Morresi Manuela, *Villa Porto Colleoni a Thiene. Architettura e committenza nel Rinascimento vicentino*, Milano 1988.

Morresi Manuela, *Jacopo Sansovino*, Milano 2000.

Palucchini Rodolfo, *Gli affreschi di Giambattista e Giandomenico Tiepolo alla Villa Valmarana di Vicenza*, Bergamo 1945.

Pasa Marco, *Villa e poderi della famiglia Rizzardi a Pojega di Negrar* in «Annuario Storico della Valpolicella 1995-1996», Vago di Lavagno 1997.

Pignatti Terisio, *Veronese. La villa di Maser*, Milano 1968.

Puppi Lionello, *La villa Badoer di Fratta Polesine*, Vicenza 1972.

Rallo Giuseppe, Fornezza Anna, *Villa Nazionale Pisani Strà*, Roma 2000.

Sandrini Arturo, *Tra "formale" e "pittoresco": il giardino Rizzardi a Pojega di Negrar* in «Annuario Storico della Valpolicella 1997-1998», Vago di Lavagno 1998.

Semenzato Camillo, *La Rotonda di Andrea Palladio*, Vicenza 1968.

Semenzato Camillo, *Villa Contarini XVI secolo. Fondazione G.E. Ghirardi. Guida alla visita*, Milano 1989.

Venuto Francesca, *Villa Manin e il suo parco. Una secolare vicenda artistica*, Tavagnacco 1995.

Villa della Torre a Fumane, a cura A. Sandrini, Cerea 1993.

For an exhaustive bibliography, please consult:

Mavian Linda, Ville Venete: bibliografia, Venezia 2001.

Photographs credits

All photographs in this volume by Cesare Gerolimetto, except aerial view of villa Manin (Passariano), page 262, by concession of Gianni D'Affara (San Daniele del Friuli, Udine).

Heartfelt thanks go to all the villa owners, who have shown their utmost kindness in allowing the author to undertake his research and the photographer to take his photographs.
The photographs of villa Contarini (Piazzola sul Brenta) are by kind concession of the Fondazione G.E. Ghirardi; of the La Badoera (Fratta Polesine) by kind concession of the Amministrazione Provinciale, Rovigo; of Villa Pisani (Stra) by kind concession of the Soprintendenza ai Beni Architettonici e per il Paesaggio del Veneto Orientale.